Creative Writings by W.E.B. Du Bois

A Pageant, Poems, Short Stories, and Playlets

THE COMPLETE PUBLISHED WORKS OF W.E.B. DU BOIS

HERBERT APTHEKER, EDITOR

813.5
D852c

Creative Writings by W.E.B. Du Bois

A Pageant, Poems, Short Stories, and Playlets

COMPILED AND EDITED BY
HERBERT APTHEKER

WITHDRAWN

LIBRARY ST. MARY'S COLLEGE

KRAUS-THOMSON ORGANIZATION LIMITED
White Plains, New York

© Copyright 1985 Kraus-Thomson Organization Limited.
Introduction © Copyright 1985 Herbert Aptheker.

All rights reserved. No part of this work covered by the copyrights hereon may be reproduced or used in any form or by any means—graphic, electronic, or mechanical, incuding photocopying, recording, or taping, or information storage and retrieval systems—without written permission of the publisher.

Materials from *The Crisis* reprinted with permission of Crisis Publishing Company.

First printing 1985

Printed in the United States of America

Library of Congress Cataloging in Publication Data

Du Bois, W.E.B. (William Edward Burghardt), 1868–1963.
  Creative writings by W.E.B. Du Bois.

  (The Complete published works of W.E.B. Du Bois)
  Bibliography: p.
  1. Blacks—Literary collections. I. Aptheker, Herbert, 1915– . II. Title. III. Series: Du Bois, W.E.B. (William Edward Burghardt, 1868–1963. Works. 1982.
PS3507.U147A6   1985   818'.5209   84-17121
ISBN 0-527-25346-4

Contents

Introduction

A Pageant

1. The People of Peoples and Their Gifts to Men — 1

Poems

2. [Paul Lawrence Dunbar: In Memoriam] — 6
3. A Litany for Atlanta — 7
4. The Song of the Smoke — 10
5. The Burden of Black Women — 12
6. My Country 'Tis of Thee — 15
7. Death — 16
8. A Day in Africa — 17
9. The Song of America — 18
10. Ave! Maria! — 19
11. The Prayer of the Bantu — 20
12. El Dorado — 21
13. A Hymn to the Peoples — 22
14. Joseph Pulitzer — 24
15. The Quadroon — 26
16. In God's Gardens — 27
17. Easter-Emancipation — 28
18. The Christmas Prayers of God — 33
19. Unrest — 37
20. Poem — 38
21. The United Nations — 39
22. [Untitled] — 40

23. The Rosenbergs 42
24. Suez 45
25. I Sing to China 47
26. Ghana Calls 52

Short Stories

27. Tom Brown at Fisk 56
28. "Wittekind" 63
29. The Case 64
30. The Shaven Lady 68
31. The Running of the Bishop 71
32. Principles 72
33. Constructive Work 73
34. The Optimist 74
35. Precept and Practice 75
36. Easter [1911] 76
37. The Woman 78
38. Jesus Christ in Georgia 79
39. A Mild Suggestion 85
40. The Third Battle of Bull Run 88
41. Easter [1913] 90
42. The Princess of the Hither Isles 91
43. The Three Wise Men 94
44. The Story of Africa 97
45. Of the Children of Peace 99
46. The Second Coming 101
47. The Flight into Egypt 103
48. Steve 104
49. The Gospel According to Mary Brown 106
50. Again, Social Equality 109
51. Of Giving Work 111
52. Clothes 112
53. Pontius Pilate 113
54. Chamounix 116
55. The Sermon in the Cradle 118
56. The Spanish Fandango 120
57. The Great Surgeon 122
58. On Being Crazy 126
59. The Gospel According to St. John, Chapter 12 128
60. Little Portraits of Africa 130
61. An Interview 133
62. The Temptation in the Wilderness 137
63. The Black Man Brings His Gifts 139

64. Georgia	146
65. The Son of God	147

Playlets

66. A Little Play	151
67. The Christ of the Andes	152

Introduction

W.E.B. Du Bois is well known for his novels, including the massive trilogy *The Black Flame,* written toward the end of his life. In addition, his immortal work *The Souls of Black Folk* is a montage of fiction and nonfiction. However, his published works outside the areas of nonfiction included a considerable body of separately issued poetry and prose. Beginning with his editorship of *The Fisk Herald* (1887–1888), during his senior year at Fisk University, Du Bois wrote and published short stories, poems, plays, and pageants. In addition, he published pieces that could best be called vignettes, which were exercises in a kind of prose portraiture that does not fall into any of the previous categories. These creative writings have never before been collected into one volume; the present work is the first such effort.

Du Bois had attempted to publish a collection of his poetry. He wrote of his effort from his teaching post at Atlanta, Georgia, in a letter dated March 29, 1943 to Frank E. Taylor, then editor-in-chief of Reynal and Hitchcock, a New York publishing firm. Du Bois here remarked that he had sent a book of poems in 1938 "to two or three publishers." He added that "all the publishers said something nice but were scared of poetry." Du Bois continued, "I nevertheless believe that this volume contains some of the best writing that I have done and touches the race problem in unusual ways."[1]

In his response, Taylor suggested that he would be interested in seeing this book of poems, but whether they were sent to him or not is unknown. Certainly, nothing further came of this exchange, and, as of this writing, the actual manuscript to which Du Bois refers has not yet been located.

In 1964, one year after Du Bois's death, a pamphlet entitled *Selected Poems* was published in Accra, Ghana. This pamphlet contained 32 pages of some of his poetry, marred by misdating and typographical errors. It included a brief foreword by President Nkrumah of Ghana, who noted: "There is evidence of bitterness and bewilderment in these lines, but there is also understanding, hope, vision, and irresistible pride of race." I visited Mrs. Du Bois in Ghana that same year; she expressed her well-merited disappointment with the effort, and decided it was not to be distributed. If any further effort was intended, the coup that came the following year certainly ended it, since it forced Mrs. Du Bois's departure from Ghana. In any case, nothing further was done along these lines.

Professor Arnold Rampersad, in a discerning essay, concludes that Du Bois "never attained complete competence as a great poet or novelist." He adds, however,

---

[1] See H. Aptheker, ed., *Correspondence of W.E.B. Du Bois,* 3 vols. (Amherst, Mass.: University of Massachusetts Press, 1973–78), 2:361–362.

that "his efforts in those roles combine with his other works to extend our understanding of the history and character of his people and, indeed, of humanism itself."[2] Both judgments are correct, I believe. In this volume, both for the record and for the enjoyment of the reader, a considerable segment of Du Bois's fantastic productivity can be found.

The effort in this volume—as in all volumes comprising *The Complete Published Works of W.E.B. Du Bois*—is for completeness. Typographical errors (they were not numerous) have been silently corrected. Where a particular work was reprinted, the original version is provided here; if later versions contained significant variations, these have been called to the reader's attention.

In a diary entry made on his twenty-fifth birthday, while a student at the University of Berlin, Du Bois pledged to devote all his energies and talents to the liberation of his people; this was to include his work in science and in art. There is no more dramatic illustration of the strengths of Du Bois's prophetic powers than this passage, meant for his eyes only.

All of his ninety-five years were devoted to this great purpose. In doing so, he also served the cause of human emancipation—as he himself became increasingly conscious as he matured. This dedication governed his approach to literature; he wanted it to be partisan and effective. For this purpose, he demanded beauty in art, truth in content, and clarity, combined with a passion in its message against oppression. Racism, colonialism, impoverishment, violence, unjust war, and the degradation of women were the targets of Du Bois's wrath; against these he devoted all his time, his boundless energy, and his genius.

Furthermore, Du Bois had great pride in, and affection for, his own people. Hence, he insisted that their art be their own, and that Black artists must produce *primarily* for Black people. Of course, Black art should not be *only* for Black people but, Du Bois insisted, it must be produced by, for, and directed mainly at Black people. He insisted that only then could it be true, be lasting, and be able to flourish. Then, too, it would be effective in the great overriding end—to advance freedom.

Poetry, wrote Du Bois in *The Pittsburgh Courier* (October 23, 1937), "is wisdom clothed in beauty: beauty in form, sound, and sheer fitness." Only in the creative presentation of truth would Black art flourish, he told the readers of *The Crisis* (June 1921).[3] In an interview in the Norfolk, Virginia, *Journal and Guide* (July 30, 1929), he insisted that Blacks must create for their own people, not for white people. When we write for our own, he explained, we write freely and for an audience that is best able to judge the worth of what we do, and the truth of what we produce. Truth was the object; only in the creative presentation of the truth would Black art flourish. This theme is repeated time and time again by Du Bois in interviews and articles.

Du Bois felt that art for art's sake was false; attempting it, he thought, was fleeing the struggle—and that was the road to betrayal and death. Reviewing Alain Locke's collection *The New Negro* in *The Crisis* (January 1926), Du Bois wrote that he disagreed with Locke's idea therein that "Beauty rather than Propaganda should be the object

---

[2] Arnold Rampersad, "Du Bois as a Man of Literature," *American Literature* (March 1979): 68.

[3] See W.E.B. Du Bois, *Book Reviews by W.E.B. Du Bois,* edited by Herbert Aptheker (Millwood, N.Y.: Kraus-Thomson Organization Ltd., 1977), pp. 78–79.

of Negro literature and art. . . . if Mr. Locke's thesis is insisted upon too much it is going to turn the Negro renaissance into decadence."

In his influential address "Criteria of Negro Art," delivered at the 1926 NAACP Conference in Chicago and published in *The Crisis* (October 1926), Du Bois insisted that "all Art is propaganda and ever must be. . . . I do not care a damn for any art that is not used for propaganda."[4] Since Blacks are the oppressed, he added, then Blacks need and can afford the Truth; Black art must be for Blacks, it must serve them, and Blacks must freely judge it.

Somewhat later, in responding to an unnamed aspiring young Black writer, Du Bois stated that such young artists faced many temptations. Of all these, the most awful was that of trying to write for a white audience, when "the chief reason for his writing" must be "the revelation of his own soul, and the picturing of his own problems and his own people" (*The Crisis,* July 1929).

* * *

Some of Du Bois's prose pieces included in this volume do not fall into any normal definition of "short story." Rather, they are vignettes, of extraordinary vision of beauty, such as "Chamounix" (1921), or of a brief autobiographical moment, such as "Little Portraits of Africa" (1924). The lovely "Steve" (1918) and the deeply moving, dramatic "The Spanish Fandango" (1922) are especially important to the full understanding of Du Bois.

Du Bois's poetry welled up from his sense of outrage at oppression and injustice, or from some particular event that evoked special horror or elation. His poetry always conveys an intensity of emotion and, at its best, has a potent impact. This is especially true of his Atlanta litany, written as he was speeding home from Alabama to be with his family as they endured the pogrom of 1906 in that Georgia city. The same sentiment permeates his lament at the execution of the Rosenbergs almost fifty years later.

No one, not Claude McKay nor Eldridge Cleaver before he was "born again," conveyed a profounder sense of anger and rebellion than did Du Bois. Some of his poetry, such as "The Burden of Black Women" (1907) and "The Song of America" (1908)—and some of his stories, such as "A Mild Suggestion" (1917)—are quite blistering in their fury.

A lighter touch is not unknown. At times, Du Bois's humor suggests a Dick Gregory performance at its best: two examples are "On Being Crazy" (1923) and "The Black Man Brings His Gifts" (1925). His satirical poem "My Country 'Tis of Thee" (1907) has the same touch.

The ideas of "Black is Beautiful" and "Black Power" came from Du Bois; one can feel the strong emotion evoked by his remarkable poem "The Song of the Smoke" (1907):

> I will be black as blackness can—
> The blacker the mantle, the mightier the man!
> . . .
> I am daubing God in night,
> I am swabbing Hell in white.

---

[4]For the actual article from *The Crisis,* see W.E.B. Du Bois, *Selections from The Crisis,* edited by Herbert Aptheker (Millwood, N.Y.: Kraus-Thomson Organization Ltd., 1983).

I do not know whether Du Bois was the first to depict Christ as Black, but he certainly did this often and early. In all of his writings, the ready use of Biblical language reflects that he was deeply read in both Testaments. However, Du Bois was not religious in a conventional sense, and he disliked organized religion. He was, however, deeply religious in that he believed in a kind of ultimate mystery in life, guided by some Creative Force; he also believed in a form of immortality. Indeed, one of his manuscripts, written during 1909–1910, was entitled "Prayers for Dark People."[5] Du Bois retained this kind of religiosity to his final days; it suffuses his poetry and his stories.

Du Bois was a poet and prophet; these related features of his genius shine through the poetry and creative prose that he published from time to time during some seven decades. These features are present in this volume; the reader will find these works to be sources of wisdom, beauty, and precious flashes of insight.

HERBERT APTHEKER

---

[5] Published with that title, edited by H. Aptheker (Amherst, Mass.: University of Massachusetts Press, 1980).

Creative Writings
by W.E.B. Du Bois

A Pageant, Poems, Short Stories, and Playlets

1

The People of Peoples and Their Gifts to Men

PRELUDE

The lights of the Court of Freedom blaze. A trumpet blast is heard and four heralds, black and of gigantic stature, appear with silver trumpets and standing at the four corners of the temple of beauty cry:

"Hear ye, hear ye! Men of all the Americas, and listen to the tale of the eldest and strongest of the races of mankind, whose faces be black. Hear ye, hear ye, of the gifts of black men to this world, the Iron Gift and Gift of Faith, the Pain of Humility and the Sorrow Song of Pain, the Gift of Freedom and of Laughter, and the undying Gift of Hope. Men of the world, keep silence and hear ye this!"

Four banner bearers come forward and stand along the four walls of the temple. On their banners is written:

"The First Gift of the Negro to the world, being the Gift of Iron. This picture shall tell how, in the deep and beast-bred forests of Africa, mankind first learned the welding of iron, and thus defense against the living and the dead."

What the banners tell the heralds solemnly proclaim.

Whereat comes the

First Episode. The Gift of Iron:
The lights grow dim. The roar of beasts is heard and the crash of the storm. Lightnings flash. The dark figure of an African savage hurries across the foreground, frightened and cowering and dancing. Another follows defying the lightning and is struck down; others come until the space is filled with 100 huddling, crowding savages. Some brave the storm, some pray to their Gods with incantation and imploring dance. Mothers shield their children, and husbands their wives. At last, dimly enhaloed in mysterious light, the Veiled Woman appears, commanding in stature and splendid in garment, her dark face faintly visible, and in her right hand Fire, and Iron in her left. As she passes slowly round the Court the rhythmic roll of tomtoms begins. Then music is heard; anvils ring at the four corners. The arts flourish, huts arise, beasts are brought in and there is joy, feasting and dancing.

From *The Crisis* 6 (November 1913): 339–341. [This pageant, produced by Charles Burroughs, was shown in October 1913 as part of the National Emancipation Exposition in New York City. A cumulative audience of about 14,000 people were able to see the pageant. Similar pageants by Du Bois were presented in Philadelphia, Washington and Los Angeles. *See* H. Aptheker, *Annotated Bibliography of Writings of Du Bois* (Millwood, N.Y.: Kraus-Thomson Organization Limited, 1973), entry nos. 565, 575, 1936, 1937.—ED.]

A trumpet blast calls silence and the heralds proclaim

The Second Episode, saying:

"Hear ye, hear ye! All them that come to know the Truth, and listen to the tale of the wisest and gentlest of the races of men whose faces be black. Hear ye, hear ye, of the Second Gift of black men to this world, the Gift of Civilization in the dark and splendid valley of the Nile. Men of the world, keep silence and hear ye this." The banners of the banner bearers change and read:

"The Second Gift of the Negro to the world, being the Gift of the Nile. This picture tells how the meeting of Negro and Semite in ancient days made the civilization of Egypt the first in the world."

There comes a strain of mighty music, dim in the distance and drawing nearer. The 100 savages thronged round the whole Court rise and stand listening. Slowly there come fifty veiled figures and with them come the Sphinx, Pyramid, the Obelisk and the empty Throne of the Pharoah drawn by oxen. As the cavalcade passes, the savages, wondering, threatening, inquiring, file by it. Suddenly a black chieftain appears in the entrance, with the Uraeus in one hand and the winged Beetle in the other. The Egyptians unveil and display Negroes and mulattoes clothed in the splendor of the Egyptian Court. The savages salaam; all greet him as Ra, the Negro. He mounts the throne and the cavalcade, led by posturing dancers and Ra, and followed by Egyptians and savages, pass in procession around to the right to the thunder of music and tomtoms. As they pass, Ra is crowned as Priest and King. While the Queen of Sheba and Candace of Ethiopia join the procession at intervals.

Slowly all pass out save fifty savages, who linger examining their gifts. The lights grow dim as Egyptian culture dies and the fifty savages compose themselves to sleep. As they sleep the light returns and the heralds proclaim

The Third Episode, saying:

"Hear ye, hear ye! All them that come to see the light and listen to the tale of the bravest and truest of the races of men, whose faces be black. Hear ye, hear ye, of the Third Gift of black men to this world—a Gift of Faith in Righteousness hoped for but unknown; men of the world, keep silence and hear ye this!" The banners change and read:

"The Third Gift of the Negro to the world, being a Gift of Faith. This episode tells how the Negro race spread the faith of Mohammed over half the world and built a new culture thereon."

There is a sound of battle. The savages leap to their feet. Mohammed and fifty followers whirl in and rushing to the right beat the savages back. Fifty Songhay enter and attack the Mohammedans. Fifty other Mohammedans enter and attack the Songhay. Turning, the Songhay bear the last group of Mohammedans back to the left where they clash with the savages. Mohammedan priests strive and exhort among the warriors. At each of the four corners of the temple a priest falls on his face and cries: "God is God! God is God! There is no God but God, and Mohammed is his prophet!" Four more join, others join until gradually all is changed from battle to the one universal cry: "God is God! God is God! There is no God but God, and Mohammed is his prophet!" In each corner, however, some Mohammedans hold slaves in shackles, secretly.

Mansa Musa appears at the entrance with entourage on horseback, followed by black Mohammedan priests and scholars. The procession passes around to the right with music and dancing, and passes out with Mohammedans and Songhay, leaving some Mohammedans and their slaves on the stage.

The herald proclaims

The Fourth Episode, saying:

"Hear ye, hear ye! All them that know the sorrow of the world. Hear ye, hear ye, and listen to the tale of the humblest and the mightiest of the races of men whose faces be black. Hear ye, hear ye, and learn how this race did suffer of Pain, of Death and Slavery and yet of this Humiliation did not die. Men of the world, keep silence and hear ye this!" The banners change again and say:

"The Fourth Gift of the Negro to the world, being a Gift of Humiliation. This gift shows how men can bear even the Hell of Christian slavery and live."

The Mohammedans force their slaves forward as European traders enter. Other Negroes, with captives, enter. The Mohammedans take gold in barter. The Negroes refuse gold, but are seduced by beads and drink. Chains rattle. Christian missionaries enter, but the slave trade increases. The wail of the missionary grows fainter and fainter until all is a scene of carnage and captivity with whip and chain and only a frantic priest, staggering beneath a cross and crowned with bloody thorns, wanders to and fro in dumb despair.

There is silence. Then a confused moaning. Out of the moaning comes the slave song, "Nobody Knows the Trouble I've Seen," and with it and through the chained and bowed forms of the slaves as they pass out is done the Dance of Death and Pain.

The stage is cleared of all its folk. There is a pause, in which comes the Dance of the Ocean, showing the transplantation of the Negro race over seas.

Then the heralds proclaim

The Fifth Episode, saying:

"Hear ye, hear ye! All them that strive and struggle. Hear ye, hear ye, and listen to the tale of the stoutest and the sturdiest of the races of men whose faces be black. Hear ye, hear ye, and learn how this race did rise out of slavery and the valley of the shadow of death. Men of the world, keep silence and hear ye this!" The banners change again and read:

"The Fifth Gift of the Negro to the world, being a Gift of Struggle Toward Freedom. This picture tells of Alonzo, the Negro pilot of Columbus, of Stephen Dorantes who discovered New Mexico, of the brave Maroons and valiant Haytians, of Crispus Attucks, George Lisle and Nat Turner."

Twenty-five Indians enter, circling the Court right and left, stealthily and watchfully. As they sense the coming of the whites, they gather to one side of the temple, watching.

Alonzo, the Negro, enters and after him Columbus and Spaniards, in mail, and one monk. They halt the other side of the temple and look about searchingly, pointing at the Indians. Slaves follow. One of the slaves, Stephen Dorantes, and the monk seek the Indians. The monk is killed and Stephen returns, circling the Court, tells his tale and dies. The Spaniards march on the Indians. Their slaves—the Maroons—revolt and march to the left and meet the Indians on the opposite side. The French, some of the mulattoes and Negroes, enter with more slaves. They march after the Spanish. Their slaves, helped by mulattoes and Toussaint, revolt and start back. The French follow the Spaniards, but the returning Haytians meet oncoming British. The Haytians fight their way through and take their place next to the Maroons. Still more slaves and white Americans follow the British. The British and Americans dispute. Attucks leads the Americans and the British are put to flight. Spanish, French and British, separated by dancing Indians, file around the Court and out, while Maroons, Haytians and slaves file around in the opposite direction and meet the Americans. As they pass the French, by guile induce Toussaint to go with them. There is a period of hesitation. Some slaves are freed, some Haytians resist aggression. George Lisle, a freed Negro, preaches the true religion as the masters listen. Peace ensues and the slaves sing at their tasks. Suddenly King Cotton arrives, followed by Greed, Vice, Luxury and Cruelty. The slave-holders are seduced. The old whips and chains appear. Nat Turner rebels and is killed. The slaves drop into despair and work silently and sullenly. The faint roll of tomtoms is heard.

The hearalds proclaim

The Sixth Episode, saying:

"Hear ye, hear ye! Citizens of New York, and learn of the deeds of eldest and strongest of the races of men whose faces be black. Hear ye, hear ye, of the Sixth and Greatest Gift of black men to the world, the Gift of Freedom for the workers. Men of New York, keep silence and hear ye this." The banners change and say:

"The sixth and last episode, showing how the freedom of black slaves meant freedom for the world. In this episode shall be seen the work of Garrison and John Brown; of Abraham Lincoln and Frederick Douglass, the marching of black soldiers to war and the hope that lies in little children."

The slaves work more and more dejectedly and drivers force them. Slave music comes. The tomtoms grow louder. The Veiled Woman appears with fire and iron. The slaves arise and begin to escape, passing through each other to and fro, confusedly. Benezet, Walker and Garrison enter, scattering their writings, and pass slowly to the right, threatened by slave drivers. John Brown enters, gesticulating. A knot of Negroes follow him. The planters seize him and erect a gallows, but the slaves seize his body and begin singing "John Brown's Body."

Frederick Douglass enters and passes to the right. Sojourner Truth enters and passes to the left. Sojourner Truth cries "Frederick, is God dead?" Voices take up the cry, repeating: "Frederick, is God dead?" Douglass answers: "No, and therefore slavery must end in blood." The heralds repeat: "Slavery must end in blood."

The roll of drums is heard and the soldiers enter. First, a company in blue with Colonel Shaw on horseback.

A single voice sings "O Freedom." A soprano chorus takes it up.

The Boy Scouts march in.

Full brasses take up "O Freedom."

Little children enter, and among them symbolic figures of the Laborer, the Artisan, the Servant of Men, the Merchant, the Inventor, the Musician, the Actor, the Teacher, Law, Medicine and Ministry, the All-Mother, formerly the Veiled Woman, now unveiled in her chariot with her dancing brood, and the bust of Lincoln at her side.

With burst of music and blast of trumpets, the pageant ends and the heralds sing:

"Hear ye, hear ye, men of all the Americas, ye who have listened to the tale of the eldest and strongest of the races of mankind, whose faces be black. Hear ye, hear ye, and forget not the gift of black men to this world—the Iron Gift and Gift of Faith, the Pain of Humility and Sorrow Song of Pain, the Gift of Freedom and Laughter and the undying Gift of Hope. Men of America, break silence, for the play is done."

Then shall the banners announce:

"The play is done!"

2

[Paul Laurence Dunbar: in Memoriam]

June 27, 1872.

Because I had loved so deeply
Because I had loved so long
God in His great compassion
Gave me the gift of song.

Because I had loved so vainly
And sung with such faltering breath
The Master in infinite mercy
Offers the boon of death.

February 9, 1906.

From *The Moon* (Memphis, Tenn.) 1:14(March 2, 1906): cover. [This issue of *The Moon* was dedicated to the distinguished poet and novelist, Paul Laurence Dunbar. The words "faltering breath" refer to the tubercular condition which afflicted Dunbar for many years.—ED.]

3

A Litany of Atlanta

O Silent God, Thou whose voice afar in mist and mystery hath left our ears a-hungered in these fearful days—
Hear us, good Lord!

Listen to us, Thy children: our faces dark with doubt, are made a mockery in Thy sanctuary. With uplifted hands we front Thy heaven, O God, crying:
We beseech Thee to hear us, good Lord!

We are not better than our fellows, Lord; we are but weak and human men. When our devils do deviltry, curse Thou the doer and the deed: curse them as we curse them, do to them all and more that ever they have done to innocence and weakness, to womanhood and home.
Have mercy upon us, miserable sinners!

And yet whose is the deeper guilt? Who made these devils? Who nursed them in crime and fed them on injustice? Who ravished and debauched their mothers and their grandmothers? Who bought and sold their crime, and waxed fat and rich on public iniquity?
Thou knowest, good God!

Is this Thy justice, O Father, that guilt be easier than innocence, and the innocent crucified for the guilt of the untouched guilty?
Justice, O Judge of men!

Wherefore do we pray? Is not the God of the fathers dead? Have not seers seen in Heaven's halls Thine hearsed and lifeless form stark amidst the black and rolling smoke of sin, where all along bow bitter forms of endless dead?
Awake, Thou that sleepest!

Thou art not dead, but flown afar, up hills of endless light, thru blazing corridors of suns, where worlds do swing of good and gentle men, of women strong and free—far from the cozeage, black hypocrisy and chaste prostitution of this shameful speck of dust!
Turn again, O Lord, leave us not to perish in our sin!

From *The Independent* (New York) 61 (October 11, 1906): 856–858. [Du Bois wrote this piece while hastening home to his family in Atlanta, Ga., after having learned of the pogrom there in the summer of 1906. At the time Du Bois was engaged in research for the U.S. Census Bureau in Alabama. Published with slight variations in *Darkwater* (New York: Harcourt, Brace, 1921; repr. Millwood, N.Y.: Kraus-Thomson Organization Limited, 1975), pp. 25-28.—Ed.]

From lust of body and lust of blood
   Great God deliver us!

From lust of powers and lust of gold,
   Great God deliver us!

From the leagued lying of despot and of brute,
   Great God deliver us!

A city lay in travail, God our Lord, and from her loins sprang twin Murder and Black Hate. Red was the midnight; clang, crack and cry of death and fury filled the air and trembled underneath the stars when church spires pointed silently to Thee. And all this was to sate the greed of greedy men who hide behind the veil of vengeance!
   Bend us Thine ear, O Lord!

In the pale, still morning we looked upon the deed. We stopped our ears and held our leaping hands, but they—did not wag their heads and leer and cry with bloody jaws: *Cease from Crime!* The word was mockery, for thus they train a hundred crimes while we do cure one.
   Turn again our captivity, O Lord!

Behold this maimed and broken thing; dear God it was an humble black man who toiled and sweat to save a bit from the pittance paid him. They told him: *Work and Rise.* He worked. Did this man sin? Nay, but some one told how some one said another did—one whom he had never seen nor known. Yet for that man's crime this man lieth maimed and murdered, his wife naked to shame, his children, to poverty and evil.
   Hear us, O heavenly Father!

Doth not this justice of hell stink in Thy nostrils, O God? How long shall the mounting flood of innocent blood roar in Thine ears and pound in our hearts for vengeance? Pile the pale frenzy of blood-crazed brutes who do such deeds high on Thine altar, Jehovah Jireh, and burn it in hell forever and forever!
   Forgive us, good Lord; we know not what we say!

Bewildered we are, and passion-tost, mad with the madness of a mobbed and mocked and murdered people; straining at the armposts of Thy Throne, we raise our shackled hands and charge Thee, God, by the bones of our stolen fathers, by the tears of our dead mothers by the very blood of Thy crucified Christ: *What meaneth this?* Tell us the Plan; give us the Sign!
   Keep not thou silent, O God!

Sit no longer blind, Lord God, deaf to our prayer and dumb to our dumb suffering. Surely Thou too are not white, O Lord, a pale, bloodless, heartless thing?
   Ah! Christ of all the Pities!

Forgive the thought! Forgive these wild, blasphemous words. Thou art still the God of our black fathers, and in Thy soul's soul sit some soft darkenings of the evening, some shadowings of the velvet night.

But whisper—speak—call, great God, for Thy silence is white terror to our hearts! The way, O God, show us the way and point us the path.

Whither? North is greed and South is blood; within, the coward, and without, the liar. Whither? To death?
Amen! Welcome dark sleep!

Whither? To life? But not this life, dear God, not this. Let the cup pass from us, tempt us not beyond our strength, for there is that clamoring and clawing within, to whose voice we would not listen, yet shudder lest we must, and it is red, Ah! God! It is a red and awful shape.
Selah!

In yonder East trembles a star.
Vengeance is mine; I will repay, saith the Lord!

Thy will, O Lord, be done!
Kyrie Eleison!

Lord, we have done these pleading, wavering words.
We beseech Thee to hear us, good Lord!

We bow our heads and hearken soft to the sobbing of women and little children.
We beseech Thee to hear us, good Lord!

Our voices sink in silence and in night.
Hear us, good Lord!

In night, O God of a godless land!
Amen!

In silence, O Silent God.
Selah!

Done at Atlanta, in the Day of Death, 1906.

4

The Song of the Smoke

I am the Smoke King
I am black!
I am swinging in the sky,
I am wringing worlds awry;
I am the thought of the throbbing mills,
I am the soul of the soul-toil kills,
Wraith of the ripple of trading rills;
Up I'm curling from the sod,
I am whirling home to God;
   I am the Smoke King
   I am black.

I am the Smoke King,
I am black!
I am wreathing broken hearts,
I am sheathing love's light darts;
   Inspiration of iron times
   Wedding the toil of toiling climes,
   Shedding the blood of bloodless crimes—
Lurid lowering 'mid the blue,
Torrid towering toward the true,
   I am the Smoke King,
   I am black.

I am the Smoke King,
I am black!
I am darkening with song,
I am hearkening to wrong!
   I will be black as blackness can—
   The blacker the mantle, the mightier the man!
   For blackness was ancient ere whiteness began.
I am daubing God in night,
I am swabbing Hell in white:
   I am the Smoke King
   I am black.

From *The Horizon* 1 (February 1907): 4–6.

>   I am the Smoke King
>   I am black!
> I am cursing ruddy morn,
> I am hearsing hearts unborn:
>   Souls unto me are as stars in a night,
>   I whiten my black men—I blacken my white!
>   What's the hue of a hide to a man in his might?
> Hail! great, gritty, grimy hands—
> Sweet Christ, pity toiling lands!
>   I am the Smoke King
>   I am black.

5

The Burden of Black Women

Dark daughter of the lotus leaves that watch
    the Southern sea,
Wan spirit of a prisoned soul a-panting to be
    free
    The muttered music of thy streams, the
        whispers of the deep
    Have kissed each other in thy name and kissed
        a world to sleep.

The will of the world is a mighty wind sweeping
    a cloud-cast sky,
And not from the east and not from the west
    knelled its soul-searing cry;
But out of the past of the Past's grey past, it
    yelled from the top of the sky;
    Crying: Awake, O ancient race! Wailing: O
        woman arise!
    And crying and sighing and crying again as a
        voice in the midnight cries;
    But the Burden of white men bore her back,
        and the white world stifled her sighs

The White World's vermin and filth:
        All the dirt of London,
        All the scum of New York;
        Valiant spoilers of women
        And conquerors of unarmed men;
        Shameless breeders of bastards
        Drunk with the greed of gold.
        Baiting their blood-stained hooks
        With cant for the souls of the simple,

From *The Horizon* 2 (November 1907): 3–5. [Reprinted in *The Crisis* 9 (November 1914). Also published as "The Riddle of the Sphinx," in *Darkwater*, pp. 53–55.—Ed.]

Bearing the White Man's Burden
Of Liquor and Lust and Lies!

———

Unthankful we wince in the East
Unthankful we wail from the westward,
Unthankfully thankful we sing,
In the un-won wastes of the wild:
I hate them, Oh!
I hate them well,
I hate them, Christ!
As I hate Hell,
If I were God
I'd sound their knell
This day!

———

Who raised the fools to their glory
But black men of Egypt and Ind?
Ethiopia's sons of the evening,
Chaldeans and Yellow Chinese?
The Hebrew children of Morning†
And mongrels of Rome and Greece?
    Ah, well!
And they that raised the boasters:
Shall drag them down again:
Down with the thefts of their thieving
And murder and mocking of men,
Down with their barter of women
And laying and lying of creeds,

Down with their cheating of childhood,
And drunken orgies of war—
    down
        down
            deep down,
Till the Devil's strength be shorn,
Till some dim, darker Davad a hoeing of his
  corn,
And married maiden, Mother of God,
Bid the Black Christ be born!

Then shall the burden of manhood.
Be it yellow or black or white,
And Poverty, Justice and Sorrow—
The Humble and Simple and Strong

Shall sing with the Sons of Morning
And Daughters of Evensong.

Black mother of the iron hills that guard the
 blazing sea,
Wild spirit of a storm-swept soul a-struggling
 to be free,
Where 'neath the bloody finger marks, thy
 river bosom quakes,
Thicken the thunders of God's voice, and lo!
 a world awakes!

EDITOR'S NOTE
†In *Darkwater* this line and the one above read:

> "Indians and yellow Chinese,
> Arabian children of morning,".

6

My Country 'Tis of Thee

Of course you have faced the dilemma: it is announced, they all smirk and rise. If they are *ultra,* they remove their hats and look ecstatic; then they look at you. What shall you do? *Noblesse oblige;* you cannot be boorish, or ungracious; and too, after all it *is* your country and you *do* love its ideals if not all of its realities. Now, then, I have thought of a way out: Arise, gracefully remove your hat, and tilt your head. Then sing as follows, powerfully and with deep unction. They'll hardly note the little changes and their feelings and your conscience will thus be saved:

>My country tis of thee,
>Late land of slavery,
>>Of thee I sing.
>
>Land where my father's pride
>Slept where my mother died,
>From every mountain side
>>Let freedom ring!
>
>My native country thee
>Land of the slave set free,
>>Thy fame I love.
>
>I love thy rocks and rills
>And o'er thy hate which chills,
>My heart with purpose thrills,
>>To *rise* above.
>
>Let laments swell the breeze
>And wring from all the trees
>>Sweet freedom's song.
>
>Let laggard tongues awake,
>Let all who hear partake,
>Let Southern silence quake,
>>The sound prolong.
>
>Our fathers' God to thee
>Author of Liberty,
>>To thee we sing
>
>Soon may our land be bright,
>With Freedom's happy light
>Protect us by Thy might,
>>Great God our King.

From *The Horizon* 2 (November 1907): 5–6.

7

Death

Strong from the North the wind sweeps on
With darkly bitter taunt; the maid
Stands motionless—her pallid form
Swathed in the cold and clinging night.

A warrior wild rides down the World,
His sword is wet with blood; his heart
Is strangely cold; his bold black face
Is set against the wraith-wreathed earth.

World and Warrior, Maid and Mist,
Met each other—met and kissed.
Wrapped in rue, the warrior died,
And the wet wind wailed again.

From *The Horizon* 2 (December 1907): 6. [Initialed. Reprinted in the New York *Evening Post* (January 3, 1908).—ED.]

8

A Day in Africa

I rose to sense the incense of the hills,
The royal sun sent crimsoned heralds to the dawn
She glowed beneath her bridal veil of mist—
I felt her heart swell while the king
Paused on the world's rough edge,
And thousand birds did pour their little hearts
To maddened melody.
I leapt and danced, and found
My breakfast poised aloft,
All served in living gold.

In purple flowered fields I wandered
Wreathed in crimson, blue and green.
My noon-tide meal did fawn about my feet
In striped sleekness.
I kissed it ere I killed it,
And slept away the liquid languor of the noon;
Then rose and chased a wild new creature
Down the glen, till suddenly
It wheeled and fetched its fangs
Across my breast. I poised my spear:
Then saw its fear-mad piteous eyes,
And gave it life and food.

The sun grew sad. I watched
The mystic moon-dance of the elves
Amid the mirth-mad laughter of the stars;
Till far away some voice did wind
The velvet trumpet of the night—
And then in glooming caves
I laid me with the lion,
And I slept.

From *The Horizon* 3 (January 1908): 5–6.

9

The Song of America

I doom, I live, I will,
I take, I lie, I kill!
I rend and rear
In deserts drear—
I build and burrow well.
With wrack and rue
I hound and hew
On founding stones in Hell:
My Temples rise
And split the Skies,
My winged wheels do tell
The woven wonders of my hand,
The witch-work of my skill!
I writhe, I rave,
I chain the Slave
I do the deed, I kill!
Now what care I
For God or Lie?
I am the great
I WILL.

From *The Horizon* 3 (February 1908): 20–21. [Reprinted in the New York *Herald-Tribune* (October 10, 1926) and in a special issue of *Palms* (Guadalajara, Mexico), 4 (October 1926); which contained poetry by Afro-Americans and was edited by Countee Cullen.—ED.]

10

Ave! Maria!

Ave! Maria!
Mother-maid pitiful
Sister of sorrows
   And daughter of men
Ave! Maria!
Mother of Miracles
Mercy made Wonderful
To thy breast Bountiful
Gather the Sorrowful
   Daughter of Sin
Ave! Maria!
Ave! Maria!
   Gather them in!

From *The Horizon* 3 (March 1908): 2.

11

The Prayer of the Bantu

Spirit of Wonder,
Daughter of Thunder,
Fire that lurks in the cavernous Sea!
Mist of the mountain,
Song of the fountain,
Mingle thy might to the guarding of me!
God of the Day,
Lord of the Way,
Fire that flames for the Child of the Sun—
Conquer the Terrible,
Vanquish the Horrible,
Rescue thy children, Adorable One!

From *The Horizon* 3 (April 1908): 3.

12

El Dorado

Picture the wide and Peaceful Ocean,
Stretched like the living emerald
Between the soft sierras and the sun:
Yonder sweeps the great Unknown,
But here the land doth hurl itself
In panting throes of cliff and crag,
Till far aloft the gnarled and blazing silver
Of its peak do cut and grip
   The sky.
Below twixt sun and sea
Stretch rolling hills and vales
Of beauty such as mortal man
Hath never seen
Since the vast vengeance
Of God's blazing sword
Swung before Paradise.
Gold is as grass;
Great golden temples
Lift their lofty heads in air;
On golden plate
The king and all his court
   Do dine;
In gold and jewels
Women walk the gilded streets,
And all the rivers pour
Their golden flood
Down the Golden Sea.

From *The Horizon* 3 (June 1908): 7–8.

13

A Hymn to the Peoples

O Truce of God!
And primal meeting of the Sons of Man,
Foreshadowing the union of the World!
From all the ends of earth we come!
Old Night, the elder sister of the Day,
Mother of Dawn in the golden East,
Meets in the misty twilight with her brood,
Pale and black, tawny, red and brown,
The mighty human rainbow of the world,
Spanning its wilderness of storm.

Softly in sympathy the sunlight falls,
Rare is the radiance of the moon;
And on the darkest midnight blaze the stars—
The far-flown shadows of whose brillance
Drop like a dream on the dim shores of Time,
Forecasting Days that are to these
As day to night.

So sit we all as one.
So, gloomed in tall and stone-swathed groves,
The Buddha walks with Christ!
And Al-Koran and Bible both be holy!

Almighty Word!
In this Thine awful sanctuary,
First and flame-haunted City of the Widened World,
Assail us, Lord of Lands and Seas!

We are but weak and wayward men,
Distraught alike with hatred and vainglory;
Prone to despise the Soul that breathes within—
High visioned hordes that lie and steal and kill,
Sinning the sin each separate heart disclaims

From *The Independent* (New York) 71 (August 24, 1911): 400; also appears in *Darkwater,* pp. 275–276. [Du Bois composed this poem on the occasion of the convention of the First All-Races Congress, held in London in July 1911.—ED.]

Clambering upon our riven, writhing selves,
Besieging Heaven by trampling men to Hell!

We be blood-guilty! Lo, our hands be red!
Not one may blame the other in this sin!
But here—here in the white Silence of the Dawn,
Before the Womb of Time,
With bowéd hearts all flame and shame,
We face the birth-pangs of a world:
We hear the stifled cry of Nations all but born—
The wail of women ravished of their stunted brood!
We see the nakedness of Toil, the poverty of Wealth,
We know the Anarchy of Empire, and doleful Death
   of Life!
And hearing, seeing, knowing all, we cry:

Save us, World-Spirit, from our lesser selves!
Grant us that war and hatred cease,
Reveal our souls in every race and hue!
Help us, O Human God, in this Thy Truce
To make Humanity divine!

14

Joseph Pulitzer
October the Twenty-ninth, 1911

Softly, quite softly—
For I hear, above the murmur of the sea,
Faint and far-fallen footsteps, as of One
Who comes from out beyond the endless
    ends of Time,
With voice that downward looms thro'
    singing stars;
Its subtle sound I see thro' these long-
    darkened eyes,
I hear the Light He bringeth on his
    hands—
Almighty Death!
Softly, oh, softly, lest He pass me by,
And that unquivering Light toward
    which my longing soul
And tortured body through these years
    have writhed,
Fade to the dun darkness of my days.

Softly, full softly, let me rise and greet
The strong, low luting of that long-
    awaited call;
Swiftly be all my good and going gone,
And this vast veiled and vanquished
    vigor of my soul
Seek somehow otherwhere its rest and
    goal,
Where endless spaces stretch,
Where endless time doth moan,
Where endless light doth pour
Thro' the black kingdoms of eternal
    death.

From the New York *World* (November 1, 1911): 10.

Then haply I may see what things I
    have not seen,
Then may I know what things I have
    not known;
Then may I do my dreams.
Farewell! No sound of idle mourning
    let there be
To shudder this full silence—save the
    voice
Of children—little children, white and
    black,
Whispering the deeds I tried to do for
    them;
While I at last unguided and alone
Pass softly, full softly.

15

The Quadroon

Daughter of Twilight,
Mothered of Midnight,
Fathered of Daylight and Dawn;
   Shadow of Sunlight,
   Shimmering Starlight,
   Sister of Forest and Fawn!

Maid of a Morrow,
Mistress of Sorrow,
Mingled of Mourning and Mirth;
   Born of World Brotherhood,
   Crowned of all Motherhood,
   Beauty of Heaven and Earth!

From *The Crisis* 3 (November 1911): cover. [Unsigned. Reprinted in *Negro History Bulletin* 34:5 (May 1971): 116.—ED.]

16

In God's Gardens

O mist-blown Lily of the North,
A-bending southward in thy bloom,
And bringing beauty silver sown
And pale blue radiance of snows—

O fair white Lily, bowing low,
Above the dream-swept poppy's mouth,
Athwart the black and crimson South—
Why dost thou fear—why dost thou fear?

Lo! sense its sleep-sown subtle breath,
Where wheel in passioned whirl above
All lingering, luring love of love—
All perfume born of dole and death.

Cold ghost-wreathed Lily of the North,
When once thy dawning darkens there,
Come then with sunlight-sifted hair
And seek the haunting heaven of Night.

Where, over moon-mad shadows whirled,
The star-tanned mists dim swathe the sky
In phantasy to dream and die—
A wild sweet wedding of the World.

From *The Crisis* 3 (April 1912): 235.

17

Easter-Emancipation
1863–1913

I am dead;
Yet somehow, somewhere,
In Time's weird contradiction, I
May tell of that dread deed, wherewith
I brought to the Children of the Moon
Freedom and vast salvation.

I was a woman born
And trod that streaming street
That ebbs and flows from Harlem's hills
Thro' caves and cañons limned in light
Down to the twisting sea.

That night of nights
I stood alone and at the End
Until the sudden highway to the Moon,
Golden in splendor
Became too real to doubt.

Dimly I set foot upon the air;
I fled, I flew, thro' thrills of light,
With all about, above, below and whirring
Of almighty wings.

I found a twilight land
Where, hardly hid, the sun
Sent softly saddened rays of
Red and brown to burn the iron earth
And bathe the snow-white peaks
In mighty splendor.

Black were the men,
Hard-haired and silent slow,
Moving as shadows

From *The Crisis* 5 (April 1913): 285–288. [Reprinted, with some changes, as "Children of the Moon" in *Darkwater*, 187–192.—ED.]

Bending with face of fear to earthward;
And women there were none.

"Woman, woman, woman!"
I cried in mounting terror.
"Woman and child!"
And the cry sang back
Thro' Heaven with the
Whirring of almighty wings.

Wings, wings, endless wings,
Heaven and earth are wings;
Wings that flutter, furl and fold,
Always folding and unfolding,
Ever folding yet again;

Wings, veiling some vast
And veiled face,
In blazing blackness,
Behind the folding and unfolding
The rolling and unrolling of
Almighty wings!

I saw the black men huddle
Fumed in fear, falling face downward;
Vainly I clutched and clawed,
Dumbly they cringed and cowered,
Moaning in mournful monotone:
   O Freedom, O Freedom,
   O Freedom over me;
   Before I'll be a slave
   I'll be buried in my grave
   And go home to my God
   And be free.

It was an angel music
From the dead,
And ever, as they sang,
The winged Thing of wings, filling all Heaven,
Folding and unfolding, and folding yet again,
Tore out their blood and entrails

'Til I screamed in utter terror
And a silence came:
A silence and the wailing of a babe.

Then at last I saw and shamed;
I knew how these dumb dark and dusky
    things

Had given blood and life
To fend the caves of underground
The great black caves of utter night
Where earth lay full of mothers
And their babes.

Little children sobbing in darkness,
Little children crying in silent pain,
Little mothers rocking and groping and
    struggling,
Digging and delving and groveling
Amid the dying-dead and dead-in-life,
And drip and dripping of warm, wet blood
Far, far beneath the wings,
The folding and unfolding of almighty
    wings.

I bent with tears and pitying hands
Above these dusky star-eyed children,
Crinkly haired, with sweet-sad baby voices
Pleading low for light and love and living
And I crooned:

> Little children weeping there,
> God shall find thy faces fair;
> Guerdon for thy deep distress,
> He shall send His tenderness;
> For the tripping of thy feet
> Make a mystic music sweet
> In the darkness of thy hair;
> Light and laughter in the air—
> Little children weeping there,
> God shall find thy faces fair!

I strode above the stricken bleeding men,
The rampart 'ranged against the skies,
And shouted:
"Up I say, build and slay;
Fight face foremost, force a way,
Unloose, unfetter and unbind;
Be men and free."

Dumbly they shrank
Muttering they pointed toward that peak
Than vastness vaster,
Whereon a darkness brooded,
"Who shall look and live," they sighed;
And I sensed
The folding and unfolding of almighty wings.

Yet did we build of iron, bricks and blood;
We built a day, a year, a thousand years.
Blood was the mortar, blood and tears
And, ah, the Thing, the Thing of wings,
The wingèd folding wing of Things,
Did furnish much mad mortar
For that tower.

Slow and ever slower rose the towering task
And with it rose the sun.
Until at last on one wild day,
Wind-whirled, cloud-swept and terrible,
I stood beneath the burning shadow
Of the peak.
Beneath the whirring of almighty wings
While downward from my feet
Streamed the long line of dusky faces
And the wail of little children sobbing under
Earth.†

"Freedom!" I cried.
"Freedom!" cried Heaven, Earth and Stars,
And a Voice near-far
Amid the folding and unfolding of Almighty
    wings
Answered "I am Freedom—
Who sees my face is free—
He and his."

I dared not look;
Downward I glanced on deep bowed heads
    and closèd eyes,
Outward I gazed on flecked and flaming
    blue—
But ever onward, upward flew
The sobbing of small voices;
Down, down, far down into the night.

Slowly I lifted livid limbs aloft;
Upward I strove: The Face, the Face;
Onward I reeled: The Face, the Face!
To Beauty wonderful as sudden death
Or horror horrible as endless life—
Up! Up! the blood-built way
(Shadow grow vaster!
Terror come faster!)
Up! Up to the blazing blackness
Of one veilèd face
And endless folding and unfolding,

Rolling and unrolling of Almighty wings:
The last step stood!
The last dim cry of pain
Fluttered across the stars—
And then—

Wings, wings, triumphant wings,
Lifting and lowering, waxing and waning,
Swinging and swaying, twirling and
    whirling,
Whispering and screaming, streaming and
    gleaming,
Spreading and sweeping and shading and
    flaming—
Wings, wings, eternal wings,
'Til the hot red blood
Thundered thro' Heaven and mine ears
While all across a purple sky
The last vast pinion
Trembled to unfold.

I rose upon the Mountain of the Moon;
I felt the blazing glory of the Sun.
I heard the Song of Children crying "Free!"
I saw the Face of Freedom—
And I died.

Editor's Note
†In *Darkwater*, the next stanza begins with the following four additional lines:

> Alone, aloft,
> I saw through firmaments on high
> The drama of Almighty God,
> With all its flaming suns and stars.

18

The Christmas Prayers of God

Name of God's Name!
Red murder reigns;
All Hell is loose;
On gold autumnal air
Walk grinning devils barbed and hoofed,
While high on hills of hate,
Black-blossomed, crimson sky'd,
Thou sittest, dumb.

Father Almighty!
This earth is mad!
Palsied, our cunning hands;
Rotten, our gold;
Our argosies reel and stagger
Over empty seas;
All the long aisles
Of Thy great temples, God,
Stink with the entrails
Of our souls.
And Thou art dumb.

Above the thunder of Thy thunders,
   Lord,
Lightening Thy lightings,
Rings and roars
The dark damnation
Of this Hell of war.
Red piles of pulp of hearts and heads,
And little children's hands.

Allah!
Elohim!†
Death is here!
Dead are the living, deep dead the dead.
Dying are earth's unborn—

From *The Crisis* 9 (December 1914); 83–84. [Reprinted, with some changes, as "The Prayers of God" in *Darkwater*, 249–252.—Ed.]

The babes' wide eyes of genius and of
   joy;
Poems and prayers, sun-glows and earth-
   songs;
Great pictured dreams,
En-marbled phantasies,‡
Hymns of high Heaven,
All fade, in this dread night,
This long ghost night—
While Thou art dumb.

Have Mercy!
Have mercy upon us, miserable sinners!
Stand forth, unveil Thy face,
Pour down the light
That seethes this devil's dance to darkness!
Hear!
Speak!
In Christ's great name—

* * *

I hear.
Forgive me, God.
Above the thunder I hearkened;
Beneath the silence, now,
I hear.

* * *

(Wait, God, a little space.
It is so strange to talk with Thee—
Alone!)

* * *

This gold?
I took it.
Is it Thine?
Forgive; I did not know.

Blood? Is it wet with blood?
'Tis from my brother's hands.
(I know; his hands are mine.)
It flowed for Thee, O Lord.

War? Not so, not war:
Dominion, Lord, and over black, not
   white.
Black, brown and fawn,
And not Thy chosen brood, O God,
We murdered.

To build Thy kingdom,
To drape our wives and little ones,
And set their souls a'glitter—
For this we killed these lesser breeds
And civilized their dead,
Raping red rubber, diamonds, cocoa,
    gold.

For this, too, once, and in Thy name
I lynched a Nigger—

> (He raved and writhed,
> I heard him cry,
> I felt the life light leap and lie,
> I watched him crackle there, on
>   high,
> I saw him wither!)

      * * *

Thou?
Thee?
I lynched Thee?*

      * * *

Awake me, God I sleep!
What was that awful word Thou saidst?
That black and riven Thing—was it
   Thee?
That gasp—was it Thine?
This pain—is it Thine?
Are then these bullets piercing Thee?
Have all the wars of all the world,
Down all dim time, drawn blood from
   Thee?
Have all the lies, and thefts, and hates—
Is this Thy crucifixion, God,
And not that funny little cross,
With vinegar and thorns?**

      * * *

Help!
I sense that low and awful cry—
Who cries?
Who weeps
With silent sob that rends and tears—
Can God sob?

Who prays?
I hear strong prayers throng by,

Like mighty winds on dusky moors—
Can God pray?

* * *

Prayest Thou, Lord, and to me?
Thou needest me?
Thou *needest* me?
Thou needest *me?*
Poor wounded Soul!
Of this I never dreamed. I thought—
Courage, God,
I come!

EDITOR'S NOTES

†In *Darkwater,* after "Elohim!" was added the line "Very God of God!"

‡In *Darkwater,* the four lines following "En-marbled phantasies," were changed to:

> High hymning heavens—all
> In this dread night
> Writhe and shriek and choke and die
> This long ghost-night—
> While Thou art dumb.

*In *Darkwater,* "Thou?/ Thee?/ I lynched Thee?" were italicized.

**In *Darkwater,* two lines were added after "with vinegar and thorns?":

> Is this Thy kingdom here, not there,
> This stone and stucco drift of dreams?

19

Unrest

O God!
    Dip down Thy hands into the flame
    ways of Thy Heavens;

Splash back the foaming clouds,
Strain out Thy Suns,
And let the stars drip through,
Upon the panting blindness of our ears.

20

Poem

O Star-kissed drifting from above,
On misty moonbeams, sunshine shod,
Dim daughter of the lips of God,
To me and angels—Thou art Love!

O Earth-dipped raining joy, and rife
With all still wonders that abide,
Ghost Mother to the Time and Tide,
To me and faery—Thou art Life.

In love and life, in wrack and ruth
A whisper on the road to hell,
High heaven's herald, ringing well
Dear Death's destruction—Thou art Truth.

From *Palms* (Guadalajara, Mexico), 4 (October 1926); 19. [This special issue of the magazine *Palms* was devoted to Afro-American poetry, and was edited by Countee Cullen. The title of Du Bois's work is as given above, and it was signed by him.—ED.]

21

The United Nations

The sun and the stars are all ringing
With song rising strong from the earth,
The hope of humanity singing
A hymn to a new world in birth.

Chorus
United Nations on the march
With flags unfurled
Together fight for victory
A free new world

Take heart all you nations swept under,
By powers of darkness that ride,
The wrath of the people shall thunder,
Relentless as time and the tide.

Chorus
As sure as the sun meets the morning
The rivers go down to the sea,
A new day for mankind is dawning,
Our children shall live proud and free.

Chorus

A one-page mimeographed sheet among Du Bois's papers (undated). [This poem was probably written in 1944 or 1945, and distributed at some meeting or assembly. In his own hand next to the title Du Bois wrote "Anthem." At the bottom in another hand is the statement, "Labor Donated."—ED.]

22

[Untitled]

Hail and Hail again
Uncounted Dead of all the Wars of all the Worlds!
Outnumbering the living
Millions to one.
Hail and farewell!
Brood of blood-clotted babies
Birthed in bitter pain.
Sired of Old Man Murder,
Mothered by the harlot, Gain!
Nursed in the crippled brains of senile Senators
On the milked gold of venal Congressmen.
Trained by Generals, tricked in tawdry tinsel,
Singing to martial music, trumpeting to drum:
March, March, Robots, March!
Kill, kill, ever kill!

Come Deaf, Blind, Dumb!
Die, die, always die!
Rot, rot, ta-ra-ra, rot!

Scream, O silent Dead,
Into whose sad and sightless faces
I stand and stare.
I feel what you felt
When Assyria quenched the first fine flame of Egypt;
I see what you saw when Greeks buried Greece beneath the Parthenon;
I hear what you heard when Rome tore down her towers and fell her endless fall.
I know what you know as America murders Asia
As Africa is pain and shame
And Europe rushes down to Hell
Shrieking with candle, book and bell.
I weep the tears you can no longer weep
For you are dead and Death is black
And I am black

From *In Battle for Peace* (New York: Masses & Mainstream, 1952), pp. 180–181.

And Blacks are red with all the blood
That Whites have shed.

If cowards die let brave men live
To face the sky.
Let all be one and one vast will
Cry: Stop, Halt, Hold!
Awake O Witless, drear and dread
Awake O Mothers of the dead
Save the World!
   Save the children and their dreams
   Save the color and the sound
   Save the form of faiths unfound
Save Civilization, soul and sod,
Save the tattered shreds of God!
War is murder, murder hate
And suicide, stupidity
Incorporate.

23

The Rosenbergs
Ethel and Michael, Robert and Julius

It was the end of a long, dark day; a day of sorrow and suffering. I was very, very weary. As the night fell and the silence of death rose about me, I sat down and lay my face in my hands and closed my eyes. I heard my own voice speaking:

    Crucify us, Vengeance of God
    As we crucify two more Jews,
    Hammer home the nails, thick through our skulls,
    Crush down the thorns,
    Rain the red bloody sweat
    Thick and heavy, warm and wet.

    We are the murderers hurling mud
    We the witchhunters, drinking blood
    To us shriek five thousand blacks
    Lynched without trial
    And hundred thousands mobbed
    The millions dead in useless war.
    But this, this awful deed we do today
    This senseless, blasphemy of birth
    Fills full the cup!
    Hail Hell and glory to Damnation!
    O blood-stained nation,
    Stretch forth your hand! Grasp it, Judge
    Wrap it in your blood-red gown;
    And Lawyer in your sheet of shame;
    Proud pardoners of petty thieves
    Cautious rabbis of just Jehovah,
    And silent priests of the piteous Christ;
    Crawl wedded liars, hide from sight,
    In the dirt of all the night,
    And hold high vigil at the dawn!
    For yonder, two pale and tight-lipped children
    Stagger across the world, bearing their dead
    There lifts a light upon the Sea
    With grim color, crooked form and broken lines;

From *Masses & Mainstream* (New York), 6 (July 1953): 10–12.

With thunderous throb and roll of drums
Alleluia, Amen!

Now out beyond the plain
Streams the thick sunshine, sheet on sheet
Of billowing light!
Above the world loom vast sombre hills
Limned in lurid lightnings;
While from beneath the hideous sickened earth,
The Sea rains up flood on flood to cleanse the heavens.
Twixt Sun and Sea,
Rises the Great Black Throne.
Sternly the pale children march on
Bearing high on their hands, Father and Mother
The drums roll until the Land quivers with pain
And slowly yawns:
The children prone bow down
They bow and kneel and lie;
They lay within the earth's deep breast
The beautiful young mother and her mate.
Straight up from endless depths
Rise then the Bearers of the Pall
Sacco and Vanzetti, old John Brown and Willie McGee.
They raise the crucified aloft.
The purple curtains of Death unwind.
Hell howls, Earth screams and Heaven weeps.

High from above its tears
Drops down a staircase from the Sun
Around it with upstretched hands,
Surge of triumph and dirge of shame,
Gather the mighty Dead:
Buddha, Mahmoud and Isaiah
Jesus, Lincoln and Toussaint
Savonarola and Joan of Arc;
And all the other millions,
In throng on throng unending, weeping, singing,
With music rising heaven-high,
And bugles crying to the sky
With trumpets, harps and dulcimers;
With inward upward swell of utter song.
Then through their ranks, resplendent robes of silken velvet,
Broidered with flame, float down;
About the curling gown
Drop great purple clouds, burgeon and enthral,
Swirl out and grandly close, until alone
Two golden feet appear,
As of a king descending to his throne.
In the great silence and embracing gloom,

We the murderers
Groan and moan:

"Hope of the Hopeless
Hear us pray!
America the Beautiful,
This day! This day!
Who was enthroned in sunlit air?
Who has been crowned on yonder stair?
Red Resurrection,
Or Black Despair?"

24

Suez

Young Egypt rose and seized her ditch
And said: "What's mine is mine!"
Old Europe sneered and cried: "The bitch
Must learn again to whine!"

The British lion up and roared
But used his nether end
Which raised a stink and made men shrink
As world peace seemed to rend.

Dull Dulles rushed about the world,
His pockets full of gold.
Ike sadly left his game of golf
And talked as he was told:

"Lord God! Send Peace and Plenty down
"And keep on drafting hen.
"Send billions east and so at least
"No income tax shall end."

Adlai essays with polished phrase
To say the same thing less
And prove without a shade of doubt
Both parties made this mess!

The campaign's done and Ike has won,
We spent ten millions for the fun.
Meantime it would be well to note
How many million did not vote.

Young Israel raised a mighty cry:
"Shall Pharaoh ride anew?"
But Nasser grimly pointed West:
"They mixed this witches' brew!"

From *Masses & Mainstream* 9 (December 1956): 42–43.

Big Three are shouting long and loud;
United Nations boil;
Big Business raves: "Drop on these waves
A million tons of oil!"

With whites withdrawn, the traffic runs
As it has run before.
But white folk fumed and pointed out
Red pilots from the shore.

Old Britain would be Great again
With War on Earth, bad will to men!
And France would civilize the dead
And make the black Sahara red.

Greed splits the West and hatreds swell
To rebuild race and color pride,
Where Moses and Mohammed died
And Jesus Christ is crucified.

Israel as the West betrays
Its murdered, mocked, and damned,
Becomes the shock troop of two knaves
Who steal the Negro's land.

Beware, white world, that great black hand
Which Nasser's power waves
Grasps hard the concentrated hate
Of myriad million slaves.

The Soviets in blood and tears
Have made their socialism strong.
The West quite frantic in its fears
Has tried to stamp it to the ground.

This cannot be, it's but the sight
Of private capital's sad plight.
Fear makes America feel free
To buy revolt in Hungary.

For eastward trumpets sing the song,
The rising sun calls loud and long.
And Africa lifts high its head,
And sees all Asia burning Red!

25

I Sing to China
Dedicated to Kuo Mo-Jo, May 1, 1959

Hail, dark brethren of mine,
Hail and farewell! I die,
As you are born again, bursting new with life.
Kith you are of mine, and kin.
That Sun which burned my fathers ebony,
Rolled your limbs in gold,
And made us both, cousins to the stars!

Farewell and Hail!
Now I turn West, where kindly Death
Opens its arms of endless sleep
Crying as I die: be born, New China,
Celestial Kingdom, Golden Realm!

Hail, China!
I go, I leave, I hasten home
Where Dulles' brink can punish a nigger,
For greeting a chink!
My country 'tis of thee,
I cannot sing.

But I can bring greetings
From six hundred eighty million souls—
Marching, pushing, pulling;
Singing, weeping, crawling to conquer
Themselves and the world.

Bursting pale bonds of poverty
Dull Ignorance, dread Disease!
Hand held in hand
Of that strong elder brother
Great Soviet Russia, Northern Light.

Emperor of all Snow and Ice;
Who, wounded and scarred from fighting half the
    World,

From *China Reconstructs* (Peking), 8 (June 1959): 6. [Du Bois, with his wife Shirley Graham, visited the People's Republic of China for several months early in 1959.—E D.]

Stands today, wise, strong and proud;
Exulting and exalted.

She who once felt Pain blasting Pain,
Blood bleeding Blood
Hope eating up Despair
But now sits aloft, unconquered and unconquerable;

Not perfect, but with her eyes firm-fixed
On Perfection!
Beckoning all her brethren: south, east and west
White and black, yellow and brown
All colors, all men!
All knowledge, all good!

Eternal China!
Live again, unending Life of Death!
Hear not the howling of the Hounds of Hell,
Old China Hands who kicked their servants;

Raped your daughters
And prostituted your wives;
Sent priest, with opium in their right hands, guns in
    their left;
Crosses on their foreheads and gin in their flasks,
To baptize the heathen!

Torment yourselves, O Chinese people,
Flagelate your souls, my brothers,
Do bitter penance for those awful years
And centuries of yielding
To self-murder, degradation and despair;
To faithfulessness to China and mankind.

Work now and struggle; sacrifice with joy,
In just requital for the cruelty and neglect,
You, yourselves, meted out to
Your mothers, wives, and children
And yourselves

Count sweat and toil today;
Hunger and cold;
Nakedness and suffering, as just pay
For centuries of surrender.

Forget the little shrimp that stinks and stews on Taiwan
Forget his dogs, Rhee and Diem.
Remember alone their ravaged peoples, the helpless
    pawns

Of blood-stained paws, of blood jaws.
Be calm; their end is written in their stars;
Even their fellow-thieves in America
Cower in defeat.

You have faced the Dragon, China,
That fearsome Beast who ruled a thousand years;
A writhing coil sin, a poison fang, a slimy horror!
Who frightened you to submission
And bound your feet and bowed your backs.

Hearken to the drums, listen to the feet:
The March, the Long Long March from Ming to
   Mao, led by the Ghost
Of Sun Yat-sen!
With the Song of Tu Fu, the memory of Confucius
   and Tao!
Sing, Liu, to the starving; starve with the song, Chou!

And Chu Teh, fight, fight, fight!
Through the snows and over the mountains,
You carry treasure;
You carry Gold, but not the Gold
Of banks and war-lords

But the fine Gold of human hearts
Whose price can never fall!
Which is scarce only as it is not used
Spend your Gold, China, scatter it and throw it abroad
Buy all mankind as you have bought me
Bought me and bound me and made me
Forever and forever yours!

Away Myth and Miracle, Greed and Dogma;
Up Science, Truth, Right and Reason
Come, Little England, dying France,
Live on your own toil and no longer on the Stolen
   land and labor.
Of slaves.
Rejoice, Honesty, God lives again!
No Christ to kill, no faith to fan
What China worships is a Man!
A workingman, who earns his food
And toils and sweats through day and night;
And tills his land with all his might;
And owns the harvest that he sows,
And winds and pulls,
And hauls and lifts
And counts his children as his gifts;

And thinks and plans,
And learns and knows;

And plants the tree and sails the sea,
And works for all and all for me;
And they for us and we for them;
Who love their fellows more than self,
And toil for others not for self.
No lofty lineage does China rear—
No lords to strut, no fools to fear
And all its myriad millions sing
Work save the people, away with kings!

Let Poet, Seer and Thinker rule,
Raise Age to honor, child to school.
To school, to school, Golden baby, China doll.
Kowtow, all sons of Heaven
To daughters of Destiny
Mothers of Men!
To the women of China
Pregnant with the fairest Future
Man ever knew!

Reach down O mighty People,
With your clenched left fist,
Grip the hands of Black Folk!
Hold fast the men from whom this world was born:

The great-brained Ape
Who stood erect and talked to his fellows
Who planted seed and first boiled Iron
And civilized a World.
Night fell, silent and noisome night, ghost-haunted,
Earthquake tore, flood roared, serpent and insect bit;
Fever raged, starvation reigned; but Africa lived;
Africa lived and grew, fared far and flourished,
Vitalized mankind.

Until the Devil rose and ruled in Europe and America,
Worshipping Greed, proclaiming God, enchaining
  His children;
Preaching Freedom, practicing Slavery
Making Africans the niggers of the World.
To be mocked and spit upon,
To be crucified! Dead and buried!
But Africa is not dead; she never died; she never will,
She writhes in sleep; this third century of her
  degradation
She struggles to awake.

Help her, China!
Help her, Dark People, who half-shared her slavery;
Who know the depths of her sorrow and humiliation;
Help her, not in Charity,

But in glorious resurrection of that day to be,
When the Black Man lives again
And sings the Song of the Ages!
Swing low, Sweet Chariot—
Good news! the Chariot's a'coming!
Then again, Peace! Then forward the World, forward
  Mankind!
No more Murder!

Ignore the memory of white men who tossed pence
  to paupers
Yoked children to machines
Ate babies in their mills
Waxed fat on profits.

Remember only the Saints of the West
John Brown and Garrison
Lincoln and Douglass
Pray that lost Britain
Live in truth as once it wanted to live
And bring back the World it murdered.

Sweet cities of China
With gold-coil roofs and curling eaves
With flaming walls and flowering gardens
And laughing children rolling in the sun,
Thunder your lightnings
From the Great Wall to Himalayas
Where pearls and jewels of Jolma Lumgna
Peer down on all the earth!

Shout, China!
Roar, Rock, roll River;
Sing, Sun and Moon and Sea!
Move Mountain, Lake and Land,
Exalt Mankind, Inspire!
For out of the East again, comes Salvation!
Leading all prophets of the Dead—
Osiris, Buddha, Christ and Mahmoud
Interning their ashes, cherishing their Good;
China save the World!
Arise, China!

26

Ghana Calls
Dedicated to Kwame Nkrumah

I was a little boy, at home with strangers.
I liked my playmates, and knew well,
Whence all their parents came;
From England, Scotland, royal France
From Germany and oft by chance
The humble Emerald Isle.

But my brown skin and close-curled hair
Was alien, and how it grew, none knew;
Few tried to say, some dropped a wonderful word
   or stray;
Some laughed and stared.

And then it came: I dreamed.
I placed together all I knew
All hints and slurs together drew.
I dreamed.

I made one picture of what nothing seemed
I shuddered in dumb terror
In silence screamed,
For now it seemed this I had dreamed;

How up from Hell, a land had leaped
A wretched land, all scorched and seamed
Covered with ashes, chained with pain
Streaming with blood, in horror lain
Its very air a shriek of death
And agony of hurt.

Anon I woke, but in one corner of my soul
I stayed asleep.
Forget I could not,

But never would I remember
That hell-hoist ghost
Of slavery and woe.

I lived and grew, I worked and hoped
I planned and wandered, gripped and coped
With every doubt but one that slept
Yet clamoured to awaken.
I became old; old, worn and gray;
Along my hard and weary way
Rolled war and pestilence, war again;
I looked on Poverty and foul Disease
I walked with Death and yet I knew
There stirred a doubt: Were all dreams true?
And what in truth was Africa?

One cloud-swept day a Seer appeared,
All closed and veiled as me he hailed
And bid me make three journeys to the world
Seeking all through their lengthened links
The endless Riddle of the Sphinx.

I went to Moscow; Ignorance grown wise taught me
   Wisdom;
I went to Peking: Poverty grown rich
Showed me the wealth of Work
I came to Accra.

Here at last, I looked back on my Dream;
I heard the Voice that loosed
The Long-looked dungeons of my soul
I sensed that Africa had come
Not up from Hell, but from the sum of Heaven's
   glory.

I lifted up mine eyes to Ghana
And swept the hills with high Hosanna;
Above the sun my sight took flight
Till from that pinnacle of light
I saw dropped down this earth of crimson, green and
   gold
Roaring with color, drums and song.

Happy with dreams and deeds worth more than doing
Around me velvet faces loomed
Burnt by the kiss of everlasting suns

Under great stars of midnight glory
Trees danced, and foliage sang;

The lilies hallelujah rang
Where robed with rule on Golden Stool
The gold-crowned Priests with duty done
Pour high libations to the sun
And danced to gods.

Red blood flowed rare 'neath close-clung hair
While subtle perfume filled the air
And whirls and whirls of tiny curls
Crowned heads.

Yet Ghana shows its might and power
Not in its color nor its flower
But in its wondrous breadth of soul
Its Joy of Life
Its selfless role
Of giving.
School and clinic, home and hall
Road and garden bloom and call
Socialism blossoms bold
On Communism centuries old.

I lifted my last voice and cried
I cried to heaven as I died:
O turn me to the Golden Horde
Summon all western nations
Toward the Rising Sun.

From reeking West whose day is done,
Who stink and stagger in their dung
Toward Africa, China, India's strand
Where Kenya and Himalaya stand
And Nile and Yang-tze roll:
Turn every yearning face of man.

Come with us, dark America:
The scum of Europe battened here
And drowned a dream
Made fetid swamp a refuge seem:

Enslaved the Black and killed the Red
And armed the Rich to loot the Dead;
Worshipped the whores of Hollywood
Where once the Virgin Mary stood
And lynched the Christ.

Awake, awake, O sleeping world
Honor the sun;

Worship the stars, those vaster suns
Who rule the night
Where black is bright
And all unselfish work is right
And Greed is Sin.

And Africa leads on:
Pan Africa!

27

Tom Brown at Fisk
In Three Chapters

CHAPTER I

Oh, she was so tired! The long road stretched on and on until it was lost in the gathering twilight. It's hard to be a woman, but a black one, —! "Mister! *Mister!*" "Who-a! Wa-al!" "Would you be so kind as to direct me to Squire Brown's house? He is the school director I believe." "Wal I don't jest ezactly know. Ain't much acquainted 'round these yere parts, but I'll tell ye, ef ye keep this yere pike fur nigh 'bout a mile an' a half p'rhaps, till ye come to whar Joe Buggs lives, you'll know the place well 'nuff, big barn and water tank, wal take down that 'ar lane next to 'im; go through the piece o' woods an' take up the big road fur 'bout two mile an' you'll come to a big white house. You as' thar an' I shouldn't wonder but if they could tell ye. How fur? O' but six or seven mile." "Could I get there to night?" "Might ef you walked fas'. Leastway you kin make it by nine." Nine o'clock in the night! The very thought made her shudder, and she looked at the sun despairingly. "Be you a school teacher?" "I might be if I could find a school." "These niggers 'round here aint much on schools. Allus fussin' an' don't know nothin'—" "Well! whose fault is it?" "Taint none o' ourn, sure, we pay mighty nigh all the taxes an' yet we give 'em two er three months schoolin' a year. 'Pears like—" "How kind in you! Good day, sir, thank you for your information." "O not 'tall, not 'tall! Humph! mighty peert nigger, hey Jack! Git up thar Ned, g'long Tom, sun mus' be bout two hours high." And the wagon rolled off down the pike throwing up clouds of dust. Up the road the little woman toiled, on and on past barn, lane, and woods, until at last weary and despairing she sat down by the roadside and let the hot tears trickle through her little brown fingers tightly clasped over her aching head. "Yes," said Mrs. Judge Snell as she rolled by in her coach, "the Negroes are *very* improvident and shiftless. There is an instance now. They had much rather sit around and sleep like that girl than to be at work. You Northeners can't appreciate until you've tried it once." And her guest, who was writing up the New South, immediately jotted down the fact that the "Negroes are making little progress." Pretty soon a black head was poked over the fence. "Lor' bress you, hun, come in de house an doan be a-settin' out yere. You will ketch yo' deff o' col'." "I– really should have" she answered, hastily wiping away the tears and looking up into the kindly old face, "I really didn't see the house." "Specs yo' didn't. Dun tole de ole man dat co'n wuz gittin so high we's all hid. Doan reckon you frum 'round dese parts, is you? Hab a cheer," as

---

From the *Fisk Herald* 5(December 1887): 5–7; 5(January 1888): 6–7; 5 (March 1888): 5–7. [The *Fisk Herald*, a student publication of Fisk University in Nashville, Tenn., was edited by Du Bois during his senior year (1887–1888).—ED.]

they came to the hut. "O no! my name is Ella Boyd. My home is in Mississippi but I've been attending school at Fisk University for about four years. My father died last year so I had to do something for myself to keep in school. I started out to find a country school to teach about three weeks ago but it seems almost hopeless:" In spite of her efforts to the contrary tears of disappointment filled her eyes. "I'se pow'ful sorry you had sich luck,—heah you Ben, go ketch dat 'ar white pullet, quick! e'r I'll war you' out Nigger! Pow'ful sorry! Guess youse de one Tom said he seed at the normal at Haywood. Tom's my oldes' boy, mighty fine 'un too! He said dar wuz a mighty peert little brownskin gal dar from de colleg, an' I 'lowed you'se de one when I seed you. Whar's you tried to git a school?" "O everywhere. First I went to Glennville, but some one was ahead of me. Then I went to Alexandria and there they had no money. I next heard of a school at Baird's Mill, but they wanted me to teach seventy children for fifteen dollars a month, and I refused; I almost wish I hadn't! Monday I went to Greensville, Buffalo Gap, and Ridges without success. This morning I went to Prosperity and was again disappointed. Being a little short of money I thought I'd walk a little way out in the country, and I walked and walked and here I am with no school yet." "Wal you'se had a hard time sho; I know youse hungry. Set right up an' hab a snack. Say blessin'?" As Ella bowed her head, she thought of the pleasant dining-room at Fisk, with its rows of pleasant faces, and she longed for the time,— "Now take out an' help yo' sef. We ain't got much but you'se welcome to what dey is. De ole man and Tom'll be here soon. Dey works ober to Squire Brown's,—" "That's the school-director isn't it?" "Yes, an' I spec's you kin git de school. You kin go up wid Tom in de mornin'. Doan reckon no one's got it git."

Pretty soon the "ole man" and Tom came, the former a perfect specimen of the good-natured old Negro farmer, the latter an awkward country lad of eighteen, nearly as dark as his mother. After supper, Mr. and Mrs. Brown, for so they were called, and Ella were soon engaged in conversation while Tom went to the rear of the house and divided his time between keeping the children quiet, and casting sly glances at the stranger. Pretty soon in spite of her efforts Ella's weary eyes would close. Mrs. Brown drove the men out doors and prepared the bed for her. "De flees am mighty bad 'round here," she explained as she turned down the dingy quilt, and the girl felt the force of her remark before morning. She had an appetizing breakfast of hot biscuits and chicken, and coffee, which the precious cook "clared wan't good 'nuff fur college folks." Ella and Tom started for the Squire's. "Do you go to school Tom?" "Yes'm, when there is any to go to." "Do you like to study?" "Yes'm." "In what reader are you?" "I was in the Fifth Reader and third-part 'rithmetic last term." "Why don't you go to Nashville to school?" "Never thought of that." "Well, just think,—". "Tom, got to hurry up here. Pile on that 'ard of corn. We must be movin'. The sun nigh on an hour high."

Tom with an awkward bound hurried on and Ella approached the old farmer. "I'm a school-teacher and I wanted to see if you had a teacher engaged here?" The old man eyed her closely and drawled out: "Well, no, but we want a man." "O, excuse me, I thought you wanted a teacher," said Ella, and calmly started to go. "Don't be in sich a hurry, pr'aps we kin make a bargain after all. Let's see your stifkit. Wal I'll be dad-jimmed ef that aint a *mighty* good 'un. Why, that's as good as *White folks.*" "Well?" "Now we've got a mighty small school and precious little money comin' to us, but I'll tell you, I'll give you fifteen dollars a month, that's as much as a woman,—" "Are you paying for women or brains?" "Wal o' course we want brains, but we got to have some 'un to keep the boys *straight.*" "I can keep them 'straight' enough. You know you wouldn't offer a white teacher such an amount." "Wal I'll give you twenty dollars, that's more'n it's worth, but I'll risk it." It was a small sum but it seemed like the last chance, and Ella accepted. Soon the contract was signed and in her pocket, and school was to open on Monday. As she passed Tom, he asked in a shy, earnest tone, "How much does it cost to go to Fisk University?"

CHAPTER II

"Who's that," said Jones of the Junior College as he reached the third floor with dust-pan and broom, and heard the rumbling of a wagon on the drive below. "Dunno" said Thomson of the Freshman, "New fellow, I reckon." "Pshaw! Thought 'twas somebody" said Jones as he jerked his head in from the window and sauntered on down to his room thinking whom he should bring out to the lecture Friday night. Thomson looked out and saw a tall, dark, awkward looking fellow, dressed in jeans, standing besides a trunk of rather ancient appearanec. A crowd of boys stood out near the bell tower cracking jokes at his expense. "Here you, dry up there, and show him up to Miss Parmelee" yelled the Freshman who was just beginning to feel his college "importance." "Better make us! Take him up yourself" was the impolite rejoinder. Thomson hurried down stairs. "Good morning. Just got in? Where are you from?" "I'm from Liberty, Tenn." "O yes. Used to teach down near there. Well, glad to see you. Let's see, what's your name?" "Tom Brown." "Know anybody here?" "Miss Boyd used to be my teacher a year or so ago." "Ella Boyd? Is that so? Why Miss Boyd is one of my *especial* friends," with a senatorial air. "Well come on up, I'll take you to the matron." After having interviewed Miss Parmelee, and encountered the Treasurer, Tom found himself ensconced on the west side of the "Buzzard Roost," (as Thomson euphoniously styled the fourth floor), with thirty-five cents in his pocket and a general feeling of lonesomeness. While prying into the mysteries of the wardrobe and bureau and examining the lamp to find out at which end to light it, he was startled by the unearthly clamor of the large bell. "What's the matter," he asked, rushing to the door. "Chapel!" yelled a boy as he rushed past tying his necktie and fell down four or five stairs in his haste. "What's them?" queried Tom anxiously. "What's *them!* Ha! ha! ha! Get your books and come on" Tom grabbed his arithmetic and Bible, and started down stairs in full gallop. "Hey, get a collar on, fellow! Ain't used to such things, are you?" howled a Prep. as Tom struck the third floor. "Keep on your foolishness' John Brown if somebody don't have to pull him oft from you" replied another as he disappeared below. At this Thomson came up and relieved the poor fellow of some of his embarrassment. "Hello, Tom! Say, boy, go upstairs and finish dressing, and I'll show you down to the chapel." Tom liked the chapel exercises very much at first, although he couldn't quite "catch on" the singing, but when he discovered Thomson making eyes at his beloved ex-school mistress, whom he had discovered after some search, somehow he felt "funny." Tom was much impressed with the marching and mentally determined to be a senior in thc van "in a mighty short while." However the Principal of the English Department soon took the larger part of his conceit away, and when with aching head he finished the mazy pile of examination papers, he was surprised to hear he had made the class.

Days and weeks passed by and Tom became gradually settled in his new surroundings, and to put on Fisk airs.

He stood a little longer before the glass, ogled the girls in prayer meetings, stood well in his studies and was actually rash enough to think of engaging company to a lecture; happily however this catastrophe was averted by Thomson who informed him patronizing that he was "too young." At first he had wanted to see Miss Boyd very much, but as the weeks rolled by and he saw so many prettier faces he soon forgot all about her nearly, except to nod as they met. However Ella was used to this for she was not pretty and consequently not overburdened with beaux (for Fiskites have a most asinine failing for faces) and she therefore had little to take her attention from her lessons except as Thomson dropped around and poured a little of his superabundant self-conceit in her ear just as though he thought (as she used to say with an angry toss of her head) she was fool enough to believe him.

The Christmas holidays soon came with their festivities, and Tom had a big box from his good old mother, visited around the city with the boys, and took part in the Mock Congress, although his active part only consisted in rising to one point of order, which sad to say was not well taken. Then came the week of prayer, and Tom, who had always viewed the wild revivals at home with a sort of contempt, was little touched. Perhaps it would not have amounted to much, had he not one day as he was passing the library heard some one call "Tom" "What?" he asked, stopping. It was Ella Boyd. "Tom" she said abruptly, after a little hesitation. "Tom, I wish you'd be a christian. You know you ought." "Ye-es." "Won't you try then?" "I don't know." "Please promise me; will you?" "Yes." "Thank you, I am so glad." And she turned away and Tom went up stairs, feeling a little queer. But he kept his word and at Wednesday night's prayer-meeting summoned up enough courage to arise and say he intended to be christian. He knew not how soon he was to be tried; it came the following afternoon in the shape of a letter. His father was dead, and his mother left alone to care for the children; he must give up his education and go home to the farm and begin his life work. Could he?

Could he leave all his schoolmates and pleasant surroundings, give up his aspirations, his longing to be a college man, and return to the now almost despised life again? It was hard bitter struggle, but the right conquered, his things were soon packed and he had bidden teachers and classmates goodbye. He lingered in the hall a moment after his last supper to bid Ella adieu; there was just a hand shake and a little later the hack was rolling to the station and Tom was no longer a Fiskite.

CHAPTER III

It was the close of the Christmas Rhetoricals. The bustling of departing visitors and students mingled with the congratulations poured upon the successful orators. One group stood near the door. You could easily recognize the affable voice of Thomson, for Thomson was a senior now, and of course—well he was a senior and every body knew it. "Who was that tall dark young man that spoke so *splendidly?*" asked one of the group, an octaroon with black waving hair and twinkling eyes, pretty, and cognizant of the fact. "Oh that was Brown. He's a freshman; this is his first time on. Smart fellow that; lost one year to take care of his mother 'till she died and then came back and not only kept up with his class, but made another. You ought to have seen him when he first came! green, whew!" "Yes, he's my chum," said another, a pretty little fellow dressed in the latest style, so that he almost looked like a laundried collar with a head on it. "Wouldn't you like to meet him?" "O yes! Do bring him here." answered Miss Floyed (the beauty), "I should like to see him ever so much." In a few moments our Tom was bowing and scraping before the group of young ladies and probably would have been blushing had not that been a physical impossibility. "Really you must come and see us" said Miss Stanley, "we live on South High." "Thank you, I will" said Tom, as visions of beauty and cake passed before his already excited brain. "Tell you, boy, you've struck a big thing. We'll have a racket in the city during the holidays," said Carter, Tom's chum, as he returned from escorting his charges to the city. "I believe Bess Floyed's stuck on you, fellow." "O pshaw! stop your nonsense" said Tom as he tucked up in the bed-clothes and industriously tried to go to sleep, which he succeeded in doing at last and dreamed that he and Miss Floyed were married and that he was the greatest orator—I don't know what else he might have dreamed had not the warning bell for breakfast started him from his slumbers. On their way from breakfast Carter imparted some very important information to Tom. "Boy, I've got an invitation for you to night at Miss Stanley's. Going to have a big time. Then next week we've something on docket for every night. I tell you, we'll just paint Nashville red; show 'em what Fiskites can do. Of course you'll need a new suit and some laundry, etc., but—" "But I haven't any money,—not a cent," said Tom dubiously. "Borrow," replied Carter sententiously as if that was a very common method with himself. "I don't like to do that." "Bah! don't get squeamish now! why, fellow, you ought to have heard Miss Floyed talking about you. Why, I tell you we'll have all these fellows opening their eyes when they see us having such a big time in the city." Tom kept thinking the matter over as he was cleaning up the room, and it must be confessed that under the ceaseless running of Carter's tongue his scruples were fast melting away. "But Miss Parmelee won't excuse us so often." "Go without an excuse then. I don't propose to be shut up here all the Christmas just because those teachers want me to be. I'm a man and propose to do as I please." "The teachers don't want you shut up here. They don't think it right however to be running out too much and staying up nights, and I don't—" "Well, you can stay here and read the Bible if you want to. Hello! there's a letter—no, a card for you. Whew! registered letter down in the office for you. Tell you, Brown, you're lucky. We can have a racket now, hey?" "Ye-es, but that money was for my school warrants and I ought to give it to Stickel." "Well I declare! You're the biggest gump-head I ever saw!" Suffice it to say that Tom took ten dollars to the Treasurer and put the remaining thirty in his pocket, and then wanted to be provoked because the Treasurer was a little gruff. Soon Tom had a new suit with a long-tailed coat, a package of laundried collars and cuffs, and countless neckties and handkerchiefs. The first two nights of eating and dancing quite turned his head, and made him deeply in love with Miss Floyed's curls. The third night the Matron flatly refused to excuse them, and they followed Carter's plan and went anyhow, for as Carter argued "they could easily get back by ten." However Carter wasn't ready to depart at that time, being engaged in a very confidential conversation with Miss Stanley, and although Tom hated to leave Miss Floyed's black eyes, he departed alone. As he crossed the railroad he saw the lights in Livingstone beginning to go out and he started out in full gallop. As he neared the bridge his foot struck a stone and he fell sprawling into one of the spacious mud-puddles which can always be found in that vicinity. Picking himself up he started out again and reached the door just in time—to find it locked. Here was a pretty fix! If he aroused the watchman he was sure to be reported, and if he didn't,—ah! here was a window left open; he crawled in, sneaked up stairs and dreamed all night that officers were arresting him for burglary. Carter turned up bright and early, in time for breakfast, and started to whisper in Tom's ear:

> Listen my children, you shall hear,
> Of the midnight run of—

but was promptly checked by a pitcher of water. Tom did not go out much the rest of the week. New Year's day however, he could not resist the temptation, especially when it was backed by a dainty missive, saying "Miss F. would be disappointed, if" &c.&c,&c. "I'm not going to buy any more cards" said Carter. "We won't need 'em." Tom readily consented for he had only fifteen cents left. They were ashamed to ask for excuses again so away they went without them. Arriving at the house they boldly rang the bell and when the door was opened by a small boy, stepped in and began to take off their over coats, when the boy held up a little server, and said, "Thirteen cards, pleth thir." Tom stood and looked at the boy for a moment and then turned just in time to see Carter's coat-tails disappearing down the street. Soon only the boy and server were left in the hall. Cards however were purchased and written in short order and often waiting long enough for the affair to be forgotten, they returned and spent the evening in most agreeable company. This time even Tom could not tear away by ten, and to make a long story short, staid out all night. "We're in for it now," said Carter as he came up stairs after breakfast, "The President wants us down in his office. He knows it all." The final result was that Carter, being an old offender, packed his trunk, while Tom received a severe reprimand, which was very effective.

It wouldn't have been so hard but when he reached his room he found a note which stated that Mr. and Mrs. John Floyed would be pleased with his company at the marriage of their daughter Bessie, to Mr. J. R. Bruce, at Louisville, Ky., Feb. 9, 188–. Tom didn't shed any tears, merely walked to the mirror and said, "Tom Brown, you're a fool!" and the young man in the mirror seemed to assent, without any mental reservations.

* * *

Ella Boyd had been compelled to lose two years for financial reasons, and was consequently a Senior Normal at the same time Tom a Senior College. They did not meet very often, for Tom's Freshman escapade had settled the girl question with him, as he thought, and he was tending strictly to his studies, while she was pursuing her quiet way as usual, not even bothered now by Thomson. The scholarship and deportment of both were very high, and once in a while they mutually sought one another's advice as to certain pet schemes. Ella had a taste for literary work and Tom's practical common-sense was often of use in toning down too brilliant passages: Tom was doing some extra work in the sciences and sometimes made her his confidant as to his future plans. Commencement soon drew near, and one day as Tom was passing the little grove in the north-west corner of Victoria square, "getting off" his oration he happened to overhear a conversation to which, being personal, he could not be blamed for listening. "That Tom Brown is just making a fool of Ella Boyd. Like to see myself running around after a boy as she does. And then he's homely as a hedge-fence—" just then Tom happened to spy Ella seated on a bench not far away, also, probably, getting the benefit of the conversation. Tom said nothing. Commencement passed off nicely. After dinner Tom spoke to Ella and asked her to take a little walk. O no, really she couldn't now she must go up stairs and pack. "I had something very important to say to you" "Well can't you say it here, Mr. Brown?" "You used to call me Tom." "I used to do a great many other foolish things" with a defiant look that said "but I don't intend to again." After considerable argument Miss Boyd was prevailed upon to take a *very* short walk. I don't know what Tom said but at any rate when Ella came back she didn't look half as mad as she *might* have, and her chum had to remind her twice not to pack the lamp in her trunk. At any rate Tom Brown is now a large farmer and stock-raiser in Kansas, worth probably ten thousand, whose christian life and example are worth many times that amount to the community, and Ella Boyd is—his wife.

28

"Wittekind"

The old hag chuckled.

The lady drew aside her skirts disdainfully and tried to look unconcerned but you see there was no one else about and one must talk. So she arranged her placket-hole complacently and said

"At last."

The old hag chuckled. The lady looked at her. She was very old and very wrinkled and very black. Her hair was crinkled and tufted and her claw-like hands folded themselves graspingly over her long staff.

"At last," resumed the lady, "they are here: six hundred white servants and laborers. We'll see Carolina white yet—an excellent month's work."

"Six months," chuckled the black hag.

"Well then, six months; what of it?" snapped the lady, patting her back hair.

"Hark!" cried the hag.

"Hark to what? O yes, hear the good ship 'Wittekind' dropping anchor."

"Hark!" chuckled the hag. A confused wailing swept the sea.

"What's that?" whispered the lady, startled.

"18,000 black babies born."

"Born when?"

"In the last six months."

"Where?"

"In Carolina!"

The lady twisted her skirts about her and without a word disappeared.

The old hag chuckled.

From *The Horizon* 1 (April 1907): 9–10.

29

The Case

I had taken the morning train at Washington for New Orleans on the Southern. I was not feeling very well and it was a dull, gray day. Few other people were foolish to ride in such unpleasant weather. I yawned and stretched—tried to look at the landscape but there wasn't any worth looking at. Then I looked at the porter. He was a finely-made fellow—tall, strong, with velvet dark brown skin and pleasant, smiling eyes. If he had been white—but he wasn't. I growled: "Won't these trains ever run on time?" But he smiled and said nothing. We left the straggling Virginia station at last and wound along slowly southward. Things seemed to grow worse—bad trains, bad food, no company. I strolled to the smoking room and lit a cigar. It was also bad. "Heavens," I said, addressing the porter again, "even a wreck would be a diversion for this sort of thing." He smiled. "I guess you've never been in a wreck," he said in excellent English. "No," I replied, "have you?" "Lots of them; one only last trip," said he. "Is that so?" said I encouragingly—but he was gone. A sickly, fussy old lady in the car wanted a softer pillow. Pretty soon he came back. "You must have a good many adventures on these trains," I said. "No, not many," he said slowly—then after a pause, "you see we get stories now and then but only parts of them, just glimpses you know." "Suppose you have to guess at the rest?" "Yes," he replied. I thought he was going at least to tell me about the wreck but as he didn't start I began again to encourage him. "Anybody killed in that wreck?" "One lady," he said, and he looked thoughtfully out the window. The little bell rang again and he went out. The fussy old lady wanted a glass of water. By and by he came back. "Have a cigar?" I said. "No thank you," he said, "against the rules." "Well tell me about that wreck," I said at last determinedly. "You see 'twas this way," he replied settling down on the arm of one of the chairs. "I was starting out of the Washington depot one morning hurrying to the train with the plan of my Pullman when a man ran against me, big, ugly-looking fellow and he cursed me when 'twas really his own fault. I turned around to him as good as he sent, when a lady standing near him said in a soft voice, 'You are going to the train?' I tell you she was a stunning-looking woman, not so very tall yet with an appearance of tallness, brunette with dark hair and the most wonderful misty eyes you ever looked at. I've seen a good many pretty women on these trains and other places but I think she was about the prettiest. She had an air, too—wasn't exactly a lady—." "What do you mean by that?" I growled. "O well, I mean she hadn't always been used to money and good society, perhaps, still she had the making of a lady in her. I don't know that I can just explain what I mean, but you perhaps understand." I did but I said nothing. He continued, "Yes ma'am," said I. 'Won't you take this bag along?' I took the bag altho it was the depot porter's work and she hurried out after

From *The Horizon* 2 (July 1907): 4–10.

me. At the gate we met a young clergyman; a tall, fresh-faced, hearty, honest-looking fellow, evidently young, and he stepped aside very courteously to let the lady have his place. It proved however that she was at the wrong gate and was not going on the Southern but on the Seaboard. I thought I noticed a little regret on the clergyman's face, she thanked me, tipped me generously and glided toward the other gate. Well it was a day something like this, cold and gray and chilly and to make it worse the train was about an hour and a half late waiting on Northern connections so that the Seaboard went and left us. The clergyman proved to be the only passenger in my car and I tell you he was lonely. He sat looking around disconsolately and in my opinion thinking of the beautiful woman he had seen at the gate. We started on down through Virginia about as fast as we are going today." "Ting-a-ling-a-ling" went the bell and off the porter went leaving me to relight my cigar. By and by he came back. I smiled, "Are women often as troublesome as this one?" "This is a mild case," he said imperturbably. "Well about dark we got to Greensboro and as I was standing outside, a veiled woman hurried toward me. 'All aboard,' the conductor shouted and the train began to quiver. I thought I recognized the figure. Sure enough it was the woman of the Washington train. How on earth could she have gotten here? Then I remembered that she could get over from Raleigh by Durham but I didn't know of any train that came at that time of night. She must have made it through some way. I seized her bag but she hesitated. 'Oh!' she said, 'have you any room in the car?' 'Plenty,' said I as I swung her up the step but she paused again. 'Are there many passengers?' 'One,' said I, 'madam.' She raised her veil and started perceptibly. 'Oh, you are the porter who carried my bag in Washington—very well,' she said and smiled as she started into the car. Of course I gave her number 7 right opposite number 6 where the clergyman was, and immediately the clergyman sat up and began to take notice. They were the only passengers in the car. He handed her a paper and then magazine, picked up her gloves and exchanged remarks about the weather, while I dusted around the seats. Pretty soon on returning from the smoking room I found them sitting together talking. Afterward they went in and had dinner together and when they came back, he was enthusiastic and she radiant. They were getting along very rapidly and I was watching them with a great deal of interest. Evidently he was much impressed and no wonder. The woman looked even more beautiful than she had in the morning. She was not only beautiful—she had a certain indefinable grace and innocence and vigor; a soft, subtle southern witchery as lovely as her accent. At the same time watching her narrowly I was not so certain about her. There was something not quite right about her and yet it struck me that she was excited, no sign of wrong in it, that she was listening for something.

Beneath all her enthusiasm and interest there were little furtive gleams almost of terror that came into her otherwise beautiful eyes, when his were turned away. Now and then a far away look of passionate pleading struggled across the very mirth of her laughter—little things, not much you know, nothing that he noticed probably but I could see—I am used to noting such things. Suddenly the train stopped, there was commotion on ahead and I went forward. When I came back the lady asked casually in tone but yet with a penetrating glance at me, 'What's the matter, porter?' 'Officers boarding the train looking for something.' She didn't say anything, yet I noticed a certain grayish whitening about her eyes, the tightening of her lips. 'Oh! go see what it is, won't you?' she said to the clergyman. He rose and hurried forward. He had scarcely reached the little passage way, when she turned suddenly to me and reaching down, took up a case; a large, leather-bound, square case. She rose stiffly and said with a sort of pleading command, 'Take this'—I supplied the rest quietly—'hide it.' 'Yes' she said looking me squarely in the eyes while a cruel harsh gleam came in hers. I bowed and stepping quickly back two sections, raised the cushion and put the case beneath the pillows, then as I was apparently brushing out the section the clergyman sauntered back. 'Oh it is nothing,' he said, 'they are searching for somebody. I don't know just what is matter.' The lady bent and made some gay remark, and then pointed out the window. He followed her finger laughingly but I wasn't fooled. I saw the dull, gray pallor creeping up her cheek. I saw the tremor in the delicate tapering of the pointed finger. I saw the flash of dull, blue steel as her other hand left her bosom. I rushed forward as there was murder or suicide in the air, when a man appeared at the entrance. 'No alarm, ladies and gentlemen,' he said, 'but we are officers and are searching the passengers on this train.' 'But,' expostulated the clergyman angrily, as he saw the dead white face of the lady, 'this is outrageous. I—.' Another official-looking personage entered—a quiet man with sharp eyes looking into every corner of the car. The clergyman glanced up and a look of recognition came over him. 'Why, hello John Travers,' he said. 'Why, Corrothers is that you?' cried the man shaking his hand heartily, 'how do you do? Why I never thought of meeting you here. This is a great pleasure. I am on a little official business—.' He glanced at the lady and hesitated. In a flash she had risen to the occasion. She looked at the clergyman with a deep blush and said demurely, 'I give you back your promise—you may introduce your—wife,' and she let her eyes fall full on his. The clergyman floundered a minute and then rose to the suggestion, 'My wife; Mr. Travers.' The other man started. 'Your wife? I beg your pardon, I didn't know you were married. I am delighted to meet Mrs. Carrothers. Why didn't you tell us, you sly dog? Well I must rush. Porter, any one else?' 'No sir,' I said. 'We won't search this car, Simmons,' he said and hurried out. I discreetly withdrew—that is into the darkness of the passage. The clergyman stood with glowing face a moment and then with a sudden gesture stretched his arms—'My wife to be,' he cried. She shuddered backward with a little gasp of pain. 'You do not understand,' she faltered. 'It was just a joke—I hated to—I could not let them search and tumble my bags.' 'I know, I know all,' he insisted, 'but make the joke a reality, a dear reality.' But her voice and face fell in misery. 'You know—nothing,' she wailed and then suddenly drew herself up. 'No,' she said, 'no!' and her face grew cold and stern. 'I—I think much, very much of you but I am not—.' He listened no longer but bending forward crushed, almost smothered her in his arms. 'Hooked,' said I, but then I saw her face. I changed my mind again. I've never seen such a curious combination of looks on a face. Surely this was no evil woman. There lay love and bewilderment, honor and yearning, beneath it trouble and fear; not perfectly written but curiously intertwined. She stepped slowly from him and sat clasping and unclasping her hands nervously. Then she bent forward and spoke rapidly but too low for me to hear, and rising quickly, her burning eyes fixed straight on mine, came rapidly toward the ladies' toilet. I was in confusion at being caught listening but she did not notice and whispered as she rustled by—'a telegraph blank, quick!' I gave it to her and she was gone but a moment and then as she glided back she slipped a bill in my hand and whispered 'Get it off, quick, for God's sake!' I swung off at the little station and gave the message, 'James Magruder, Charlotte. Safe—meet me at train. Rosalyn'. The train started. I swung back on but the porter in the next called and I went to help him. 'Charlotte', cried the train hand. I rushed toward my car, entered, seized the hidden case and hurried to the land. She stood white and still and a great tear was wandering down her cheek. Then it happened."

"What happened?" I asked. "The wreck. Quickly, suddenly as it always happens, crashing, grinding, and twisting. I saw a great long bar of timber crash through the side window and crush her down in all her splendid young beauty and grind her between the seats while the car jolted and screamed. I turned and hid my face and the clergyman staggered limp and white into the opposite section. There was a long silence. Just then a man burst into the car. I recognized him in the minute. It was the same tall rough fellow who had run against me in the Washington depot. He saw the dead body of the lady, ran quickly towards her, looked at her, glanced around and knelt down by her side. The clergyman rose, the stranger too and they faced each other silently looking across the dead body. Then the stranger saw the case in my hand. He rushed and seized it. I did not resist—I was too puzzled. Just then the train crew came in and there was confusion and moving about. I saw the stranger passing out. 'Got a match?' he said. I handed him one and that was the last I saw of him." I waited a moment. "Well?" said I. "That's all," said the porter. "All?" I cried. "Yes." "Was the girl dead?" "Yes." "And the clergyman?" "I never saw him again." "How about that case?" "I never saw that again or heard of it." "What was in it?" "I don't know," said the porter. "You know, as I told you, we only get pieces of stories on a train, they never finish themselves."

"Ting-a-ling-a-ling," said the bell.

30

The Shaven Lady

"Well, where is my watch?" I said sitting up straight and fumbling first in one vest pocket and then in the other. The porter looked at me with sharp, unsmiling eyes. I found the watch soon after. It was in my upper coat pocket where I sometimes put it when I stay on a sleeping car. "Oh, I didn't think you had it," I said looking at him with a smile: he said nothing but his velvet eyes twinkled.

"You know a porter is supposed to steal everything that is missing on a Pullman car," he said. "Yes, I presume so," I replied, "were you ever accused?" "Ever?" he said, "nearly every other trip." Then he corrected himself. "No, not quite as bad as that but at least a dozen times a year something is missing and some one looks at me suspiciously; I remember one case—." But just then he was called away. Indeed it was a busy day and we had little chance to talk. At last night came; he had tucked every one in bed, even the conductor, and midnight had struck. I was not sleepy, so I went into the smoking room and lay back in one of the wicker chairs. After a time he came in, stretched himself easily on the couch and lighted a delicate cigarette. I noticed his long, thin, brown hand; beautiful fingers he had, then that voice of his—I'd give anything to hear him talk. He started.

"They got aboard the train," he said, "at Cincinnati. I was then running on the Queen and Crescent and Southern, from Cincinnati to Florida. Well as I was saying, they got aboard at Cincinnati. He was a middle-aged man, a fairly prosperous merchant I should say, with hair that was growing a little gray, an honest but rather hard face, corpulent and fairly well dressed. His daughter was not pretty and yet she was an attractive girl. I suppose eighteen or twenty, with brown hair, and smooth skin—an average American girl." He paused as he puffed away at his cigarette. "My theory is that a girl that is not very pretty is after all apt to make a man the more foolish about her. She has a certain individuality in looks. If you fall in love with a beautiful girl, why there is always a chance of your falling in love with one still more beautiful; but if you fall in love with a homely girl or a girl that is only passable, she is apt to have a monopoly in her line of looks and you'll scarcely find just her style again: at any rate, that's my theory," he said. "Well, they got aboard and I could see tears in her eyes and I knew something was wrong. They had no sooner settled themselves in their section when he began to talk. Of course it was none of my business, yet I hovered about. That's all a porter has to do, you know—did lots of dusting in the next section and had to pass pretty often. Undoubtedly he was giving her a good moral lecture. 'I tell you, Dolly,' he said, 'it's foolishness. The boy never could take care of you. He can't take care of himself. You are young yet, you haven't seen the world. I

From *The Horizon* 2 (August 1907): 5–10.

am not going to let you spoil your life this way.' The girl said little in reply but looked now miserable, now defiant.

"We rushed on down the valley and I had nearly all my time taken up in waiting on a prim and fussy old lady who sat in the section next to the man and his daughter. She wanted everything you could think of and some things almost unthinkable. She was especially put out because at Lexington a tall, rather large woman entered the Pullman and took the upper berth in her section. The lady fumed about it privately to me and the conductor all day. Were there no other upper berths? Were there none in the next car? Why should some one be crowded in with her? Meantime the tall lady, veiled and spectacled, was apparently quite unconscious of the fussy old party and sat quietly looking out the window. We had gone but a few miles when I saw her raise her veil in order to look at the scenery which was growing more wild and beautiful. Then as she turned half way from the window, a little look of recognition came into her eyes, and she smiled and bowed to the daughter sitting opposite the old gentleman. The young woman started and then looked very much perturbed. I passed on down the aisle and when I came back I found the new comer speaking to the young lady, and the old gentleman glad to have found that his daughter had run across an acquaintance, was giving his seat to her and afterward went to the smoking room. He was evidently pleased to be rid of his unpleasant charge for a while. The tall woman sat down with the young woman and gave her a hearty kiss, while the young woman's face flamed red and tears came into her eyes. I saw immediately that there was going to be an interesting exchange of confidences, but I didn't have time to watch it because the old party in the next section being relieved of the direct presence of the woman began to fume and fuss afresh. She lost her spectacles, called for water and wanted a succession of clean pillow cases. I brushed out her section several times, picked up the waste paper and orange peel and brought four glasses of water." He paused a moment as he relighted his cigarette. We could hear the sway and roar of the train. The wind whistled in the great valley by our side. It was a wild sort of night and for a moment we listened to it attentively.

"I like the roar of a running train," he said, "I'm never quite contented unless I am on one," and he looked thoughtfully out of the dark window. I said nothing; I did not like to interrupt his story. "Well," he said at last, "the day wore on and I didn't get a chance to rest until late in the afternoon, when I made what I vowed would be the last change of pillow cases the old lady would get that night. I had started away to the linen closet, when the tall lady returned to her section and bent over her bag. 'Porter,' she said, 'please take this to the dressing room for me.' I stuffed the soiled pillow case in my pocket and followed her with the bag. Once there she slipped a dollar in my hand and said, 'please deliver this quickly—he's in the car next the diner!' It was a note for the 'Rev. John Dumont'. I took it, found the genial clergyman and delivered it. He looked surprised but sent no answer. Returning I just reached my car when the old lady suddenly reared bolt upright. 'Porter,' she cried, 'conductor, where is my purse?' The whole car listened and the car conductor hurried to her. 'It was right here on the seat when the porter changed my pillow,' she declared. The conductor of course knew me. Together we searched the section thoroughly; no purse to be found. 'It had $500 and my ticket', she spouted. 'Search the porter,' suggested a drummer officiously, but I looked at him and he cooled. Just then a faint suspicion entered my head and I whispered to the conductor; together we went softly to the ladies' dressing room. I opened the door suddenly. 'Er—beg pardon—did you say the car next the diner?' I asked innocently. She gave a smothered 'yes' and banged and locked the door. I nearly fell into the conductor's arms.

" 'She's *shaving*,' I blurted out. He started and we both knew we had the thief cornered. We stood a moment irresolute in the passage, when out sweeps the lady cool and collected. 'Has dinner been called?' she asked sweetly. 'Yes, madam,' I said drily, while the conductor reached for a telegraph blank. She bent over the daughter who responded with a laugh and a blush and together they went chatting toward the dining car. We hadn't expected this move and were nonplussed. 'Are you sure?' asked the conductor balancing the blank. I simply pointed to the mannish shoulders and the suspiciously abundant hair. 'But the girl knows her,' he argued, 'and I know the girl's father well. Wait a minute; I'll ask him.' He hurried back through the car ineffectually seeking to pacify the old lady, and reached the smoking room.

" 'I beg pardon, sir,' said the conductor, 'but the lady with your daughter is an acquaintance of yours, is she not?' 'Yes, or rather of my daughter's—a former teacher.'

"I gasped. The conductor added apologetically, 'O—I—we are in a little difficulty,' and he told of the theft. 'Well you don't suppose?' said the old man angrily. Then I had to put in a word. 'But, sir, we discovered her—shaving.' The man started, dropped his paper and knitted his brows. 'Nonsense' he said but he made for the door. 'She's gone to the diner,' I said. 'O yes, she said so,' he muttered and he hurried after her. The diner was three cars back. In the third car I naturally looked for the clergyman and saw that he was just starting for the diner too. I waited outside and soon the father came hurrying in. 'The woman's not in there,' he said, 'my daughter says she returned to her car to get her purse.' I winked at the conductor and the old man seemed aroused and suspicious too. 'Come,' he said, 'we must find her.' Back we went to the car, the lady was not to be found and the old lady nearly mobbed us.

" 'She's jumped the train!' cried the conductor excitedly, as he escaped the onslaught, mopping his brow. 'Not so fast,' said the old man. 'Porter, you go back to the diner and keep your eye on that end of the train. Conductor, we'll search this train.' Back I flew. I rushed in. There stood the daughter hand in hand with a slim pale young man and the clergyman was saying, 'Do you, Dolly, take this man, Alfred, to be your wedded husband?' The sweat started on my face. I helplessly fumbled for my handkerchief. What was this wadded in my pocket? O yes it was the old lady's soiled pillow case and I jerked it out and with it out tumbled—a pocket book. I just crumpled into a chair. 'Whom God hath joined together let no man put asunder,' said the clergyman smoothly. Just then the diner door burst open and in came the father with a brown wig and mannish coat in his hand and the conductor with a silk shirt waist and a skirt.

"There was a pause. 'Here's the purse,' I said to the conductor with a sickly smile. 'I found it—in my pocket.' He looked at me and his jaw dropped, then he thoughtfully slipped the purse into the pocket of the shirt waist.

" 'Thank you for preserving my apparel,' said the young husband jauntily.

" 'Father.' cried the daughter pleadingly. But the father's face was old and grey. 'Poor foolish little girl,' he faltered."

31

The Running of the Bishop

(The reporter was two blocks and an interview behind.) And the Bishop ran. Lawn sleeves and silk gown flew and fluttered in the wind. His upturned eyes sought the starry heavens. "Help, Lord!" he gasped as great beads of perspiration gathered on his broad, white brow, and he strove mightily with the dust and gloom. Visions of angry white faces spurred him, sounds of mocking, cursing voices gave wings to his feet. The office of the *Richmond Rhymes* loomed before him. He sped down the corridor, whirled up the stairs and fell panting on the horns of the editor's altar. The editor leapt to his feet:

"The Bishop of Lon—," he began. "Sh!" "—of Lusitania," gasped the Bishop, thinking of the record just broken.

"Certainly, certainly!" assented the Editor, feelingly, "How can I serve your Grace?" and he turned—

"Thank you," whispered the Bishop feebly as he set down the cut glass—

"You know—ah—that nigger bishop!"

"Yes—Ferguson?"

"Well, Potter's dined him!"

The editor's mane rose straight up and sparkled. He was sublime—magnificent in his fury. Great staring headlines flashed in his eyes: "We'll crucify the da—"

"But wait. Potter, said, jokingly—to me—wouldn't I have dined too if—"

"Ah!" howled the delighted editor, "I see—you flayed him, you withered him, you upheld Southern—"

"Why—er—yes," fluttered the Bishop, "that is—I would—I did—I didn't—I didn't know your reporter was there!"

The editor frowned, "I see—you—"

But the prelate proceeded eagerly: "Yes, yes, I said, No—no, I said. Yes, that is, I lied, I mean I didn't mean to lie, I lied too mean, I mean I tried or at least I tried to mean—"

"—and was taken unawares?" suggested the editor, grasping his blue pencil firmly, but thoughtfully.

"Precisely; it—all too, precisely, it—" sobbed the bishop appealingly, as the triumphant reporter shot in.

The stern eyes of the editor transfixed the young man. Slash! slash! scrape! "There!" he said "I've impaled Potter and explained you." The bishop smiling feebly, wrung the editor's hand, and sank back in the cushions. *"Nunc dimittis!"* he murmured.

From *The Horizon* 2 (November 1907): 7–8.

32

Principles

The Eminent Philanthropist entered the suburban street car and appropriated the best seat. Then he looked about and spied Me.

"My Friend," he said, after greetings, "My dark and dear Friend, you are impatient. You are Over-Anxious and Ultra-Sensitive. Suppose your Rights are at times invaded, suppose you are not treated as you think you deserve—what of it? Look up, look out, look forward! Give up your right to Vote, don't insist on entrance to Theatres and Concerts, don't crowd into the Best Streets, be glad of Caste Schools all these are little things; Seek the greater; enjoy God's bounty in sun, air and beauty. Forget your Rights, do your Duty, don't complain, suffer and wait, let the abstract principle go and seize the concrete present advantage,—"

Here the conductor reaches his grimy paw for a second fare. The Eminent Philanthropist withers him with a glance.

"I have already paid, Sir—as I was saying—what? Two fares for this short distance? A new rule? Well Sir, it is an outrage. I'll not pay it—do you hear, Sir? *I'll not pay it*. It is deception, theft, highway robbery. Impatient? It is time to get impatient with these grasping stealing corporations. Moreover, Sir, I demand more respect from you—your tone is insolent. I'm *not* sensitive but I am a gentleman and demand treatment of one. *Very* well, I *will* get off. I stand upon my Rights, Sir! Damn the nickel, I don't care a rap for it—it's the Principle, Sir, the *Principle*." And the Emminent Philanthropist got off and walked.

From *The Horizon* 5 (December 1909): 1–2.

33

Constructive Work

The White Man looked contemptuously down upon the Black Leader who smiled back affably. "Get out of here," yelled the White Man as he kicked the Black Leader down stairs and tossed a quarter after him. The Black Leader pirouetted and bumped and rolled until he landed sprawling in the dirt. The dark and watching crowd were breathless, and one of them grasped his club and bared his arm. Slowly the Black Leader arose and his Eager Supporter assiduously brushed off his pants. Then the Black Leader squared his shoulders and looked about him. He cleared his throat and the throng hung upon his word breathless, eager, while the one man clutched his club tighter.

"My friends," said the Black Leader, "the world demands constructive work: it dislikes pessimists. I want to call your attention to the fact that this White gem'man—I mean gentleman—did *not* kick me nearly as hard as he might have: again he wore soft kid boots, and finally I landed in the dirt and not on the asphalt. Moreover," continued the Black Leader as he stooped in the dust, "I am twenty-five cents in." And he walked thoughtfully away, amid the frantic plaudits of the crowd. Except one man. He dropped his club and whispered:

"My God!"

From *The Horizon* 5 (December 1909): 2.

34

The Optimist

"There's nothing I hate like a Pessimist," said the White Man as he helped himself to a few public Coal Mines.

"Yes, sir," said the Black Man with big eyes.

"Pessimism," continued the White Man as he reached over and relieved the Black Man's folks of a few hundred thousand bales of cotton at $137.00 a bale, "ruined Rome and it's going to ruin this country if you don't look out."

"Yes, sir," said the Black Man, admiringly rolling his eyes at the cotton.

"Why, Sam," asked the White Man as he appropriated two railroads and raised the rates, "look at me—am I pessimistic? Do I complain?"

"No, sir," said the Black Man, and in reply the White Man reached over and took the Black Man's dinner.

"I'd asked you to join me," said the White Man as he ate it up, "but I do not believe in social equality—particularly with such a small fried chicken as this. To continue," lighting a cigar which he had smuggled, "you Niggers complain too much. I don't complain. I take what the Lord sends," and he pointed languidly to where his men were barrelling a couple of new oil wells, "and am thankful. Now I'll tell you what I'll do. If you'll go to your people and tell them to shut up and work for me for nothing and be happy, if you do this I'll make you the Boss Negro of the whole gang."

"Yes, sir," said the Black Man, "but 'spose they kicks, and talks back?"

"Pshaw," said the White Man, corralling a few daily papers, "don't I own the Associated Press?"

The Black Man just dropped on his knees, and whispered: "Here am I, send me!"

From *The Horizon* 5 (February 1910): 2.

35

Precept and Practice

A large audience was leaving New York's finest theatre. The play had been upon the Negro question, and one couple had been especially thrilled by the fine heroism of the white man, who, finding that he had a few drops of colored blood, allied himself with the despised race. "How magnificent," they were saying, "to dedicate oneself to the cause of the oppressed!"

Walking a few blocks they turned into a restaurant. After giving their order they noticed a man, a mulatto in coloring, enter and seat himself at a table. Presently a waiter came to him and whispered something. The man shook his head, and the waiter went to the proprietor.

"I really believe," the couple said, watching curiously, "that they are going to ask that man to leave. What a shame, for he is quite light and very good looking."

The proprietor came to the man as he sat at the table, and after a few words, the couple amusing themselves guessing their import, the colored man rose and left.

"That was too bad, wasn't it," one said to the other, "and right here in our own city. Perhaps the poor fellow really needed a meal," and they went on placidly enjoying their own.

From *The Crisis* 1 (December 1910): 27.

36

Easter

The land lay smiling in spring splendor, heavy with verdure, gleaming with glad sunshine. Athwart it fell the dark shadow of a toiling man; he was great of limb and black, thick of countenance and hard-haired. His face was half-hopeless, half-vacant, with only a faint gleam of something dead and awakening deep in his deep-set eyes. His feet were chained, his neck yoked and his body scarred. They that had driven him and ridden and thrust him threateningly through the thick forest were now afraid of him. They feared the reproach of his dumb, low-burning eyes. They feared the half-articulate sounds from his moving lips, and saw with terror the slow, steady growth of his body, the great, black, undying body. So they took council together to kill him—lying to his ears, crucifying his soul, until he, bent and bowed and heavy with his own weakness, fell and lay his mighty length in stupor along the earth. And the earth trembled.

Sweating and deep of breath the pale-faced murderers worked and delved, digging a cavernous grave and walling it with Oppression. Then shame-faced, yet grim, they turned northward. At daybreak they stood upon the hills of God with faces white and good, crying: "Come, O brothers, Northern brothers, the Thing that hindered our love is dead, dead, long dead." The brothers of the North came trooping, oily tongued, unctuous and rich. Yet they of the North and South looked not each other in the eye, but slunk along false-smiling.

One timid one said:

"O Brother South—I hear chains."

But the South answered:

"Nay, that is the chiming of Negro school bells."

Yet another, quibbling, found his mouth:

"Did the Thing—die—happy?"

The South choked and muttered:

"Happy—so happy—and praising his—Master, and his Best Friends."

"But, Brother, your hands are bloody," quavered a third.

"The blood of the offering burned at the stake for the culture and supremacy of the White Race."

Then hastily the South said in chorus as if to forestall reply:

"See where we have laid Him," and they pointed to that grave, walled with Oppression.

But suddenly the World was wings and the voice of the Angel of the Resurrection beat like a mighty wind athwart their ears, crying:

"He is not here—He is risen."

From *The Crisis* 1 (April 1911): 20.

Risen above half his ignorance; risen to more than six hundred millions of property; risen to a new literature and the faint glimmering of a new Art; risen to a dawning determination to be free; risen to a newer and greater ideal of Humanity than the world has known. RISEN!

37

The Woman

In the land of the Heavy Laden came once a dreary day. And the King who sat upon the Great White Throne raised up his eyes and saw afar off how the hills around were hot with hostile feet, and the sound of the mocking of his enemies struck anxiously on the King's ears, for the King loved his enemies. So the King lifted up his hand and in the glittering silence spake softly, saying, "Call the servants of the King." Then the herald stepped before the armpost of the throne and cried: "Thus saith the High and Mighty One, whose name is Holy: the servants of the King." Now, of the servants of the King there were a hundred and forty-four thousand—tried men and brave, brawny of arm and quick in wit; aye, too, and women of wisdom and marvelous in beauty and grace. And yet on this drear day when the King called their ears were thick with the dust of the enemy, their eyes were blinded with the flashing of his spears, and they hid their faces in dread silence and moved not, even at the King's behest. So the herald called again. And the servants cowered in very shame, but none came forth. But the third blast of the herald struck upon a woman's heart, afar. And the woman straightway left her baking and sweeping and the rattle of tins. And the woman straightway left her chatting and gossiping and the sewing of garments. And the woman stood before the King, saying, "The servant of thy servants, O Lord."

Then the King smiled—smiled wondrously, so that the setting sun burst through the clouds and the hearts of the King's men dried hard within them. And the low-voiced King said, so low that even they that listened heard not well: "Go smite me mine enemies that they cease to do evil in my sight." And the woman quailed and trembled. Three times she lifted up her eyes unto the hills and saw the heathen whirling onward in their rage. And seeing she shrank—three times she shrank and crept to the King's feet. "O King," she cried, "I am but a woman," and the King answered: "Go then, mother of men." And the woman said, "Nay, King, but I am still a maid." Whereat the King cried: "O Maid made Man, thou shall be Bride of God." And yet the third time the woman shrank at the thunder in her ears, and whispered: "Dear God, I am black." And the King spake not, but swept the veiling of his face aside and lifted up the light of his countenance upon her and lo! it was black.

So the woman went forth on the hills of God to do battle for the King on that drear day in the land of the Heavy Laden, when the heathen raged and imagined a vain thing.

From *The Crisis* 2 (May 1911): 12. [Also published as "The Call" in *Darkwater*, pp. 161–162.—ED.]

38

Jesus Christ in Georgia

The convict guard laughed.

"I don't know," he said, "I hadn't thought of that—"

He hesitated and looked at the stranger curiously. In the solemn twilight he got an impression of unusual height and soft dark eyes.

"Curious sort of acquaintance for the Colonel," he thought; then he continued aloud: "But that nigger there is bad; a born thief and ought to be sent up for life; is practically; got ten years last time—"

Here the voice of the promoter talking within interrupted; he was bending over his figures, sitting by the Colonel. He was slight, with a sharp nose.

"The convicts," he said, "would cost us $96 a year and board. Well, we can squeeze that so that it won't be over $125 apiece. Now, if these fellows are driven, they can build this line within twelve months. It will be running next April. Freights will fall fifty per cent. Why, man, you will be a millionaire in less than ten years."

The Colonel started. He was a thick, short man, with clean-shaven face, and a certain air of breeding about the lines of his countenance; the word millionaire sounded well in his ears. He thought—he thought a great deal; he almost heard the puff of the fearfully costly automobile that was coming up the road, and he said:

"I suppose we might as well hire them."

"Of course," answered the promoter.

The voice of the tall stranger in the corner broke in here:

"It will be a good thing for them?" he said, half in question.

The Colonel moved. "The guard makes strange friends," he thought to himself. "What's this man doing here, anyway?" he looked at him, or rather, looked at his eyes, and then somehow felt a warming toward him. He said:

"Well, at least it can't harm them—they're beyond that."

"It will do them good then," said the stranger again. The promoter shrugged his shoulders.

"It will do us good," he said.

But the Colonel shook his head impatiently. He felt a desire to justify himself before those eyes, and he answered:

"Yes, it will do them good; or, at any rate, it won't make them any worse than they are."

Then he started to say something else, but here sure enough the sound of the automobile breathing at the gate stopped him and they all arose.

"It is settled, then," said the promoter.

From *The Crisis* 3 (December 1911): 70–74. [Reprinted, with some changes, as "Jesus Christ in Texas" in *Darkwater*, pp. 123–133.—Ed.]

"Yes," said the Colonel, signing his name and turning toward the stranger again.

"Are you going into town?" he asked with the Southern courtesy of white man to white man in a country town. The stranger said he was.

"Then come along in my machine. I want to talk to you about this."

They went out to the car. The stranger as he went turned again to look back at the convict. He was a tall, powerfully built black fellow. His face was sullen, with a low forehead, thick, hanging lips, and bitter eyes. There was revolt written about the mouth, and a hangdog expression. He stood bending over his pile of stones pounding listlessly.

Beside him stood a boy of twelve, yellow, with a hunted, crafty look. The convict raised his eyes, and they met the eyes of the stranger. The hammer fell from his hands.

The stranger turned slowly toward the automobile, and the Colonel introduced him. He could not exactly catch the foreign-sounding name, but he mumbled something as he presented him to his wife and little girl, who were waiting. As they whirled away he started to talk, but the stranger had taken the little girl into his lap, and together they conversed in low tones all the way home.

In some way, they did not exactly know how, they got the impression that the man was a teacher, and of course he must be a foreigner. The long cloaklike coat told this. They rode in the twilight through the half-lighted town, and at last drew up before the Colonel's mansion, with its ghostlike pillars.

The lady in the back seat was thinking of the guests she had invited to dinner, and wondered if she ought not to ask this man to stay. He seemed cultured, and she supposed he was some acquaintance of the Colonel's. It would be rather a distinction to have him there, with the Judge's wife and daughter and the Rector. She spoke almost before she thought:

"You will enter and rest awhile?"

The Colonel and the little girl insisted. For a moment the stranger seemed about to refuse. He said he was on his way North, where he had some business for his father in Pennsylvania. Then, for the child's sake, he consented. Up the steps they went, and into the dark parlor, and there they sat and talked a long time. It was a curious conversation. Afterward they did not remember exactly what was said, and yet they all remembered a certain strange satisfaction in that long talk.

Presently the nurse came for the reluctant child, and the hostess bethought herself:

"We will have a cup of tea—you will be dry and tired."

She rang and switched on a blaze of light. With one accord they all looked at the stranger, for they had hardly seen him well in the glooming twilight. The woman started in amazement and the Colonel half rose in anger. Why, the man was a mulatto, surely—even if he did not own the Negro blood, their practised eyes knew it. He was tall and straight, and the coat looked like a Jewish gabardine. His hair hung in close curls far down the sides of his face, and his face was olive, even yellow.

A peremptory order rose to the Colonel's lips, and froze there as he caught the stranger's eyes. Those eyes, where had he seen those eyes before? He remembered them long years ago—the soft tear-filled eyes of a brown girl. He remembered many things, and his face grew drawn and white. Those eyes kept burning into him, even when they were turned half away toward the staircase, where the white figure of the child hovered with her nurse, and waved good-night. The lady sank into her chair and thought: "What will the Judge's wife say? How did the Colonel come to invite this man here? How shall we be rid of him?" She looked at the Colonel in reproachful consternation.

Just then the door opened and the old butler came in. He was an ancient black man with tufted white hair, and he held before him a large silver tray filled with a china tea service. The stranger rose slowly and stretched forth his hands as if to bless the viands. The old man paused in bewilderment, tottered and then, with sudden gladness in his eyes, dropped to his knees as the tray crashed to the floor.

"My Lord!" he whispered, "and My God!" But the woman screamed:

"Mother's china!"

The doorbell rang.

"Heavens! Here is the dinner party!" exclaimed the lady.

She turned toward the door, but there in the hall, clad in her night clothes, was the little girl. She had stolen down the stairs to see the stranger again, and the nurse above was calling in vain. The woman felt hysterical and scolded at the nurse, but the stranger had stretched out his arms, and with a glad cry the child nestled in them. "Of such," he whispered, "is the Kingdom of Heaven," as he slowly mounted the stairs with his little burden.

The mother was glad; anything to be rid of the interloper even for a moment. The bell rang again, and she hastened toward the door, which the loitering black maid was just opening. She did not notice the shadow of the stranger as he came slowly down the stairs and paused by the newel post, dark and silent.

The Judge's wife entered. She was an old woman, frilled and powdered into a caricature of youth, and gorgeously gowned. She came forward, smiling with extended hands, but just as she was opposite the stranger, a chill from somewhere seemed to strike her, and she shuddered and cried: "What a draft!" as she drew a silken shawl about her and shook hands cordially; she forgot to ask who the stranger was. The Judge strode in unseeing, thinking of a puzzling case of theft.

"Eh? What? Oh—er—yes—good-evening," he said, "good-evening."

Behind them came a young woman in the glory of youth, daintily silked, with diamonds around her fair neck, beautiful in face and form. She came in lightly, but stopped with a little gasp; then she laughed gaily and said:

"Why, I beg your pardon. Was it not curious? I thought I saw there behind your man"—she hesitated ("but he must be a servant," she argued)—"the shadow of wide white wings. It was but the light on the drapery. What a turn it gave me—so glad to be here!" And she smiled again. With her came a tall and haughty naval officer. Hearing his lady refer to the servant, he hardly looked at him, but held his gilded cap and cloak carelessly toward him; the stranger took them and placed them carefully on the rack.

Last came the Rector, a man of forty, and well clothed. He started to pass the stranger, stopped and looked at him inquiringly.

"I beg your pardon," he said, "I beg your pardon, I think I have met you?"

The stranger made no answer, and the hostess nervously hurried the guests on. But the Rector lingered and looked perplexed.

"Surely I know you; I have met you somewhere," he said, putting his hand vaguely to his head. "You—you remember me, do you not?"

The stranger quietly swept his cloak aside, and to the hostess' unspeakable relief moved toward the door.

"I never knew you," he said in low tones, as he went.

The lady murmured some faint excuse about intruders, but the Rector stood with annoyance written on his face.

"I beg a thousand pardons," he said to the hostess absently. "It is a great pleasure to be here—somehow I thought I knew that man. I am sure I knew him, once."

The stranger had passed down the steps, and as he went the nurse-maid, lingering at the top of the staircase, flew down after him, caught his cloak, trembled, hesitated, and then kneeled in the dust. He touched her lightly with his hand and said, "Go, and sin no more."

With a glad cry the maid left the house with its open door and turned north, running, while the stranger turned eastward to the night. As they parted a long low howl rose tremulously and reverberated through the town. The Colonel's wife within shuddered.

"The bloodhounds," she said. The Rector answered carelessly.

"Another one of those convicts escaped, I suppose; really, they need severer measures." Then he stopped. He was trying to remember that stranger's name. The Judge's wife looked about for the draft and arranged her shawl. The girl glanced at the white drapery in the hall, but the young officer was bending over her, and the fires of life burned in her veins.

Howl after howl rose in the night, swelled and died away. The stranger strode rapidly along the highway and out into the deep forest. There he paused and stood waiting, tall and still. A mile up the road behind him a man was running, tall and powerful and black, with crime-stained face, with convict's stripes upon him and shackles on his legs. He ran and jumped in little short steps, and the chains rang. He fell and rose again, while the howl of the hounds rung harder behind him.

Into the forest he leaped and crept and jumped and ran, streaming with sweat; seeing the tall form rise before him, he stopped suddenly, dropped his hands in sullen impotence and sank panting to the earth. A bloodhound shot into the woods behind him, howled, whined and fawned before the stranger's feet. Hound after hound bayed, leapt and lay there; then silent, one by one, with bowed head, they crept backward toward the town.

The stranger made a cup of his hands and gave the man water to drink, bathed his hot head, and gently took the chains and irons from his feet. By and by the convict stood up. Day was dawning above the treetops. He looked into the stranger's face, and for a moment a gladness swept over the stains of his face.

"Why, you're a nigger, too," he said.

Then the convict seemed anxious to justify himself.

"I never had no chance," he said furtively.

"Thou shalt not steal," said the stranger.

The man bridled.

"But how about them? Can they steal? Didn't they steal a whole year's work and then, when I stole to keep from starving—" he glanced at the stranger. "No, I didn't steal just to keep from starving. I stole to be stealing. I can't help stealing. Seems like when I sees things I just must—but, yes, I'll try!"

The convict looked down at his striped clothes, but the stranger had taken off his long coat—and put it around him, and the stripes disappeared. In the opening morning the black man started toward the low log farmhouse in the distance, and the stranger stood watching him. There was a new glory in the day. The black man's face cleared up and the farmer was glad to get him.

All day he worked as he had never worked before, and the farmer gave him some cold food toward night.

"You can sleep in the barn," he said, and turned away.

"How much do I get a day?" asked the man.

The farmer scowled:

"If you'll sign a contract for the season," he said, "I'll give you ten dollars a month."

"I won't sign no contract to be a slave," said the man doggedly.

"Yes, you will," said the farmer, threateningly, "or I'll call the convict guard." And he grinned.

The convict shrunk and slouched to the barn. As night fell he looked out and saw the farmer leave the place. Slowly he crept out and sneaked toward the house. He looked into the kitchen door. No one was there, but the supper was spread as if the mistress had laid it and gone out. He ate ravenously. Then he looked into the front room and listened. He could hear low voices on the porch. On the table lay a silver watch. He gazed at it, and in a moment was beside it, with his hand on it. Quickly he slipped out of the house and slouched toward the field. He saw his employer coming along the highway. He fled back stealthily and around to the front of the house, when suddenly he stopped. He felt the great dark eyes of the stranger and saw the same dark, cloaklike coat, where he was seated on the doorstep talking with the mistress of the house. Slowly, guiltily, he turned back, entered the kitchen and laid the watch where he had found it; and then he rushed wildly with arms outstretched back toward the stranger.

The woman had laid supper for her husband, and going down from the house had walked out toward a neighbor's. She was gone but a little while, and when she came back she started to see a dark figure on the doorsteps under the tall red oak. She thought it was the new Negro hand until he said in a soft voice:

"Will you give me bread?"

Reassured at the voice of a white man, she answered quickly in her soft Southern tones:

"Why, certainly."

She was a little woman. Once she had been handsome, but now her face was drawn with work and care. She was nervous, and was always thinking, wishing, wanting for something. She went in and got him some cornbread and a glass of cool, rich buttermilk, and then came out and sat down beside him. She began, quite unconsciously, to tell him about herself—the things she had done, and had not done, and the things she had wished. She told him of her husband, and this new farm they were trying to buy. She said it was so hard to get niggers to work. She said they ought all to be in the chain gang and made to work. Even then some ran away. Only yesterday one had escaped.

At last she gossiped of her neighbors; how good they were and how bad.

"And do you like them all?" asked the stranger.

She hesitated.

"Most of them," she said; and then, looking up into his face and putting her hand in his as though he were her father, she said:

"There are none I hate; no, none at all."

He looked away and said dreamily:

"You love your neighbor as yourself?"

She hesitated—

"I try—" she began, and then looked the way he was looking; down under the hill, where lay a little, half-ruined cabin.

"They are niggers," she said briefly.

He looked at her. Suddenly a confusion came over her, and she insisted, she knew not why—

"But they are niggers."

With a sudden impulse she rose, and hurriedly lighted the lamp that stood just within the door and held it above her heard. She saw his dark face and curly hair. She shrieked in angry terror, and rushed down the path; and just as she rushed down, the black convict came running up with hands outstretched. They met in midpath, and before he could stop he had run against her, and she fell heavily to earth and lay white and still. Her husband came rushing up with cry and oath:

"I knew it," he said, "it is that runaway nigger." He held the black man struggling to the earth, and raised his voice to a yell. Down the highway came the convict guard with hound and mob and gun. They poured across the fields. The farmer motioned to them.

"He—attacked—my wife," he gasped.

The mob snarled and worked silently. Right to the limb of the red oak they hoisted the struggling, writhing black man, while others lifted the dazed woman. Right and left as she tottered to the house she searched for the stranger, with a sick yearning, but the stranger was gone. And she told none of her guests.

"No—no—I want nothing," she insisted, until they left her, as they thought, asleep. For a time she lay still listening to the departure of the mob. Then she rose. She shuddered as she heard the creaking of the limb where the body hung. But resolutely she crawled to the window and peered out into the moonlight; she saw the dead man writhe. He stretched his arms out like a cross, looking upward. She gasped and clung to the window sill. Behind the swaying body, and down where the little, half-ruined cabin lay, a single flame flashed up amid the far-off shout and cry of the mob. A fierce joy sobbed up through the terror in her soul and then sank abashed as she watched the flame rise. Suddenly whirling into one great crimson column it shot to the top of the sky and threw great arms athwart the gloom until above the world and behind the roped and swaying form below hung quivering and burning a great crimson cross.

She hid her dizzy, aching head in an agony of tears, and dared not look, for she knew. Her dry lips moved:

"Despised and rejected of men."

She knew, and the very horror of it lifted her dull and shrinking eyelids. There, heaven-tall, earth-wide, hung the stranger on the crimson cross, riven and bloodstained with thorn-crowned head and pierced hands. She stretched her arms and shrieked.

He did not hear. He did not see. His calm dark eyes all sorrowful were fastened on the writhing, twisting body of the thief, and a voice came out of the winds of the night, saying:

"This day thou shalt be with me in Paradise!"

39

A Mild Suggestion

They were sitting on the leeward deck of the vessel and the colored man was there with his usual look of unconcern. Before the seasickness his presence aboard had caused some upheaval. The Woman, for instance, glancing at the Southerner, had refused point blank to sit beside him at meals, so she had changed places with the Little Old Lady. The Westerner, who sat opposite, said he did not care a—, then he looked at the Little Old Lady, and added in a lower voice to the New Yorker that there was no accounting for tastes. The Southerner from the other table broadened his back and tried to express with his shoulders both ancestors and hauteur. All this, however, was half forgotten during the seasickness, and the Woman sat beside the colored man for a full half hour before she noticed it, and then was glad to realize that the Southerner was too sick to see. Now again with sunshine and smiling weather, they all quite naturally reverted (did the Southerner suggest it?) to the Negro problem. The usual solutions had been suggested: education, work, emigration, etc.

They had not noticed the back of the colored man, until the thoughtless Westerner turned toward him and said breezily: "Well, now, what do you say? I guess you are rather interested." The colored man was leaning over the rail and about to light his cigarette—he had several such bad habits, as the Little Old Lady noticed. The Southerner simply stared. Over the face of the colored man went the shadow of several expressions; some the New Yorker could interpret, others he could not.

"I have," said the colored man, with deliberation, "a perfect solution." The Southerner selected a look of disdain from his repertoire, and assumed it. The Woman moved nearer, but partly turned her back. The Westerner and the Little Old Lady sat down. "Yes," repeated the colored man, "I have a perfect solution. The trouble with most of the solutions which are generally suggested is that they aggravate the disease." The Southerner could not help looking interested. "For instance," proceeded the colored man, airily waving his hand, "take education; education means ambition, dissatisfaction and revolt. You cannot both educate people and hold them down."

"Then stop educating them," growled the Southerner aside.

"Or," continued the colored man, "if the black man works, he must come into competition with whites—"

"He sure will, and it ought to be stopped," returned the Westerner. "It brings down wages."

From *The Crisis* 3 (January 1912): 114–115. [It is relevant to note that Du Bois sailed to England to attend the first All-Races Congress in 1911. A similar "mild suggestion" by Du Bois can be found in "The Problem of Problems," *Inter-Collegiate Socialist* 6 (December 1917–January 1918): 5–9.—ED.]

"Precisely," said the speaker, "and if by underselling the labor market he develops a few millionaires, how now would you protect your residential districts or your select social circles or—your daughters?"

The Southerner started angrily, but the colored man was continuing placidly with a far-off look in his eyes. "Now, migration is both costly and inhuman; the transportation would be the smallest matter. You must buy up perhaps a thousand millions' worth of Negro property; you must furnish some capital for the masses of poor; you must get some place for them to go; you must protect them there, and here you must pay not ony higher wages to white men, but still higher on account of the labor scarcity. Meantime, the Negroes suddenly removed from one climate and social system to another climate and utterly new conditions would die in droves—it would be simply prolonged murder at enormous cost.

"Very well," continued the colored man, seating himself and throwing away his cigarette, "listen to my plan," looking almost quizzically at the Little Old Lady; "you must not be alarmed at its severity—it may seem radical, but really it is—it is—well, it is quite the only practical thing and it has surely one advantage: it settles the problem once, suddenly, and forever. My plan is this: You now outnumber us nearly ten to one. I propose that on a certain date, shall we say next Christmas, or possibly Easter, 1912? No, come to think of it, the first of January, 1913, would, for historical reasons, probably be best.† Well, then, on the first of January, 1913, let each person who has a colored friend invite him to dinner. This would take care of a few; among such friends might be included the black mammies and faithful old servants of the South; in this way we could get together quite a number. Then those who have not the pleasure of black friends might arrange for meetings, especially in 'white' churches and Young Men's and Young Women's Christian Associations, where Negroes are not expected. At such meetings, contrary to custom, the black people should not be seated by themselves, but distributed very carefully among the whites. The remaining Negroes who could not be flattered or attracted by these invitations should be induced to assemble among themselves at their own churches or at little parties and house warmings.

"The few stragglers, vagrants and wanderers could be put under careful watch and ward. Now, then, we have the thing in shape. First, the hosts of those invited to dine should provide themselves with a sufficient quantity of cyanide of potassium, placing it carefully in the proper cups, and being careful not to mix the cups. Those at church and prayer meeting could choose between long sharp stilettos and pistols—I should recommend the former as less noisy. Those who guard the colored assemblies and the stragglers without should carefully surround the groups and use Winchesters. Then, at a given signal, let the colored folk of the United States be quietly dispatched; the signal might be a church bell or the singing of the national hymn; probably the bell would be best, for the diners would be eating."

By this time the auditors of the colored man were staring; the Southerner had forgotten to pose; the Woman had forgotten to watch the Southerner; the Westerner was staring with admiration; there were tears in the eyes of the Little Old Lady, while the New Yorker was smiling; but the colored man held up a deprecating hand: "Now don't prejudge my plan," he urged. "The next morning there would be ten million funerals, and therefore no Negro problem. Think how quietly the thing would be settled; no more bother, no more argument; the whole country united and happy. Even the Negroes would be a great deal happier than they are at present. Instead of being made heirs to hope by education, or ambitious by wealth, or exiled invalids on the fever coast, they would all be happily ensconced in Heaven. Of course, I admit that at first the plan may seem a little abrupt and cruel, and yet is it more cruel than present conditions, and would it not be well to be a little more abrupt in our social solutions? At any rate think it over," and the colored man dropped lazily into his steamer chair and felt for another cigarette.

The crowd slowly dispersed; the Southerner chose the Woman, but was heard to say something about fools. The Westerner turned to the New Yorker and said; "Now, what in hell do you suppose that darky meant?" But the Little Old Lady went silently to her cabin.

EDITOR'S NOTE
†This date marked the fiftieth anniversary of the Emancipation Proclamation.

40

The Third Battle of Bull Run

It is just south of Manassas where Beauregard had his supplies, and east of the first two battlefields, with their ghastly relics and calm and guardian mountains.

This third battlefield is dotted with buildings green and red. A little flying engine pants continuously with its water burden, and to and fro pass dark graceful girls and sturdy brown-faced boys. There are green lawns and little trees, and westward in a hidden grotto, a grove green golden, echoing with the voices of new graduates long gone. The dull crimson building in the midst—Howland Hall—stands sturdily with a certain quietude, flinging a long, low wing modestly behind it, where sprites and gnomes and fairies dart in and out and to and fro in busy work.

Southward the girls are clustered, northward the boys, and round about are teachers' families often new founded with new and cunning babies, albeit one and the prettiest fled, suddenly, and left a sorrow underneath the trees. Teachers there are, varicolored, sunny and sad, but quiet all, busy and happy, eager and glad. With them and not above them is the principal with his boy face and his wife who has wings—wings finely frayed with beating at the bars of life—but wings withal, and in her eyes dreams.

But the battle? Ah, yes, the battle, the third and blood-bought battle of this winding brook that whimpers 'twixt the mountains and the sea; the blood of wounded souls lies along the gold green of that campus—the hail of the iron that enters thuds through the thick dark skins. Now and then the bitter stifled wail of the dying breaks the sudden stillness, then the ranks close and the school moves on.

It's clostly, this fighting. Costly in blood and men, costly in money, costliest in worry and apprehension. Each year, each month, the Forager goes North:

"A man to see you, sir."

"Who?" snorts Wall Street, wheeling in his chair.

"Colored man—begging, I think, sir."

"Another Nigger school! Give him $5 and send him on."

And the Forager pockets his shame and moves wearily to the West.

"Yes? Well, I'm giving so much to colored people already—what is this school?"

"Manassas Industrial School? Yes. And for colored youth? Yes? I never heard of it. I give to things I hear of—Battle? I thought the war was over; it isn't. How sad. Good-day."

Thus in drippings of the rich and pennies of the poor each year $18,000 is raised

---

From *The Crisis* 4 (July 1912): 132.

to dig the trench and fire the fuse and strengthen the soul in this third struggle at Manassas.

Who is fighting? North and South, black and white, rich and poor? Oh, no—more primal, more stupendous is this struggle of worlds; light and leading and industry against darkness and hate and the Devil-of-things-that-be. And who wins? God wins—or is ever about to win, if only the Forager staggers home with the food to feed the weary watchers in the trenches, the black-sweated fighters in the fields. Pity the Forager, my brothers, and hold up his hands!

Sunset on the battlefield, and the hard breathing of them that rest from their labors; to the West, glory; to the East, the moon; between, shadows of things that were and are to be; around, a rose-grown porch, the patter of little feet, Woman-with-wings, Man-who-is-ever-young, and laughter.

Up from the earth come voices, heavy with sorrow:
"O brother you must bow so low,
"O brother you must bow so low,
"For long is the way to the ever bright world,
"Let the Heaven light shine on me!"

And so on till we sleep; in our ears the soft low panting of the engine catching its breath; in our eyes the everlasting stars.

41

Easter

Lift up your heads, O ye gates and be ye lifted up, ye everlasting doors; and the King of glory shall come in.

Who is the King of glory? The Friend strong and faithful; the Friend faithful in little.

The Friend that seeks neither place nor pay; the Friend that does not boast nor blame, but sits beside us patiently; the Friend who in our weakness knows and in our travail understands; the Friend to whom, we need not say our suffering, for he has suffered even as we and with his stripes we are healed.

The Friend who looks into our tired eyes and laughs cheeringly, who grasps our hand warmly and is silent; who says: "Well done, old man," and "Good work, little sister!"

The Friend who is no impossible god or simpering angel, but human like us, hungry as we are and disappointed; who smokes and drinks with us and walks beneath the stars.

The Friend that hath clean hands and a pure heat; who hath not lifted up his soul into vanity nor sworn deceitfully.

Yes, and the Friend who, looking back through jeweled tears, has gone down the Way of Shadows to the place that is silent and dark.

Lift up your heads, O ye gates; even lift them up, ye everlasting doors; and the King of glory shall come in.

Who is this King of glory? The Faithful Friend—he is the King of glory. Selah!

From *The Crisis* 5 (April 1913): 289.

42

The Princess of the Hither Isles

Her soul was very beautiful, wherefore she kept it veiled in lightly laced Humility and Fear, out of which peered anxiously ever and anon the white and blue and pale gold of her face—beautiful as daybreak or as the laughing of a child. She sat in the Hither Isles, well walled between the This and Now, upon a low and silver throne and leaned upon its armposts sadly looking upward toward the sun. Now the Hither Isles are flat and cold and swampy, with drear drab light and all manner of slimy, creeping things, and piles of dirt and clouds of flying dust and sordid scraping and feeding and noise.

She hated them; and ever as her hands and busy feet swept back the dust and slime, her soul sat silent, silver throned, staring toward the great hill to westward, which shone so brilliant golden beneath the sunlight and above the sea.

The sea moaned and with it moaned the Princess' soul, for she was lonely; very, very lonely, and full weary of the monotone of life. So she was glad to see a moving in Yonder Kingdom on the mountain side where the sun shone warm, and when the King of Yonder Kingdom, silken in robe and golden crowned, warded by his hound, walked down along the restless waters and sat beside the armpost of her throne, she wondered why she could not love him and fly with him up the shining mountain's side out of the dirt and dust that nested between This and Now. She looked at him and tried to be glad, for he was bonny and good to look upon, this King of Yonder Kingdom: tall and straight, thin lipped and white and tawny. So again this last day she strove to burn life into his singularly sodden clay—to put his icy soul aflame wherewith to warm her own, to set his senses singing. Vacantly he heard her winged words, staring and curling his long mustaches with vast thoughtfulness. Then he said:

"We've found more gold in Yonder Kingdom."

"Hell seize your gold!" blurted the Princess.

"No—it's mine," he maintained stolidly.

She raised her eyes. "It belongs," she said, "to the Empire of the Sun."

"Nay—the sun belongs to us," said the King calmly, as he glanced to where Yonder Kingdom blushed above the sea. She glanced, too, and a softness crept into her eyes.

"No, no," she murmured, as with hesitating pause she raised her eyes above the sea, above the hill, up into the sky where the sun hung silent, splendid. Its robes were heaven's blue, lined and broidered in living flame, and its crown was one vast jewel

---

From *The Crisis* 6 (October 1913): 285, 288–289. [Reprinted, with some changes, in *Darkwater*, pp. 75–80.—ED.]

glistening in glittering glory that made the sun's own face a blackness—the blackness of utter light. With blinded, tear-filled eyes she peered into that formless black and burning face and sensed in its soft, sad gleam unfathomed understanding. With sudden wild abandon she stretched her arms toward it appealing, beseeching, entreating, and lo!

"Niggers and dagoes," said the King of Yonder Kingdom, glancing carelessly backward and lighting in his lips a carefully rolled wisp of fragrant tobacco. She looked back, too, but in half-wondering terror, for it seemed—

A Beggar man was creeping across the swamp, shuffling through the dirt and slime. He was little and bald and black, rough clothed, sooted with dirt and bent with toil. Yet withal something she sensed about him, and it seemed—

The King of Yonder Kingdom lounged more comfortably beside the silver throne and let curl a tiny trail of light blue smoke.

"I hate Beggars," he said, "especially brown and black ones." And he then pointed at the Beggar's retinue and laughed—an unpleasant laugh welded of contempt and amusement. The Princess looked and shrank on her throne. He the Beggar man was—was what? But his retinue, that squalid, sordid particolored band of vacant, dull-faced filth and viciousness, was writhing over the land, and he and they seemed almost crouching underneath the scorpion lash of one tall skeleton that looked like Death, and the twisted woman whom men call Pain. Yet they all walked as One.

The King of Yonder Kingdom laughed, but the Princess shrank on her throne and the King seeing her took a gold piece from out his purse and tossed it carelessly to the passing throng. She watched it with fascinated eyes—how it rose and sailed and whirled and struggled in the air; then seemed to burst, and upward flew its sunlight and its sheen and downward dropped its dross. She glanced at the King, but he was lighting a match. She watched the dross wallow in the slime, but the sunlight fell on the back of the Beggar's neck and he turned his head.

The Beggar, passing afar, turned his head, and the Princess straightened on her throne; he turned his head, and she shivered forward on her silver seat; he looked upon her full and slow and suddenly she saw within that formless black and burning face the same soft, sad gleam of utter understanding seen so many times before. She saw the suffering of endless years and endless love that softened it. She saw the burning passion of the sun and with it the cold unbending duty-deeds of upper air. All she had seen and dreamed of seeing in the rising, blazing sun she saw now again, and with it myriads more of human tenderness, of longing and of love. So then she knew. So then she rose as to a dream come true with solemn face and waiting eyes.

With her rose the King of Yonder Kingdom, almost eagerly.

"You'll come?" he cried. "You'll come and see my gold?" And then in sudden generosity he added: "You'll have a golden throne—up there, when we marry."

But she, looking up and on with radiant face, answered softly: "I come."

So down and up and on they mounted; the black Beggar and his cavalcade of Death and Pain, and then a space; and then a lone black hound that nosed and whimpered as he ran, and then a space; and then the King of Yonder Kingdom in his robes, and then a space; and last the Princess of Hither Isles, with face set sunward and lovelight in her eyes.

And so they marched and struggled on and up through endless years and spaces, and ever the black Beggar looked back past Death and Pain toward the maid, and ever the maid strove forward with lovelit eyes, but ever the great and silken shoulders of the King of Yonder Kingdom rose between the Princess and the sun like a cloud of storms.

Now finally they neared unto the hillside's topmost shoulder, and there most eagerly the King bent to the bowels of the earth and bared its golden entrails—all green and gray and rusted—while the Princess strained her pitiful eyes aloft to where the Beggar, set 'twixt Death and Pain, whirled his slim back against the glory of the setting sun and stood, sombre in his grave majesty, enhaloed and transfigured, outstretching his long arms; and, around all Heaven, glittered jewels in a cloth of gold.

A while the Princess stood and moaned in mad amaze, then with one wilful wrench she bared the white flowers of her breast and snatching forth her own red heart held it with one hand aloft while with the other she gathered close her robe and poised herself.

The King of Yonder Kingdom looked upward quickly, curiously, still fingering the earth, and saw the offer of her bleeding heart.

"It's a Nigger," he growled darkly; "it may not be."

The woman quivered.

"It's a Nigger," he repeated fiercely. "It's neither God nor Man, but a Nigger."

The Princess stepped forward.

The King grasped his great sword and looked north and east; he raised his long sword and looked south and west.

"I seek the sun," the Princess sang, and started into the west.

"Never!" cried the King of Yonder Kingdom, "for such were blasphemy and defilement and the making of all evil."

So raising his great sword he struck with all his might and more. Down hissed the blow and bit that little white heart-holding hand till it flew armless and disbodied up through the sunlit air. Down hissed the blow and clove the whimpering hound till his last shriek shook the stars. Down hissed the blow and rent the earth. It trembled, fell apart and yawned to a chasm wide as earth from Heaven, deep as hell, and empty, cold and silent.

On yonder distant shore blazed the mighty Empire of the Sun in warm and blissful radiance; while on this side, in shadows cold and dark, gloomed the Hither Isles and the hill that once was golden but now was green and slimy dross; all below was the sad and moaning sea, while between the Here and There flew the severed hand and dripped the bleeding heart.

Then up from the soul of the Princess welled a cry of dark despair—such cry as only babe-raped mothers know, and murdered loves. Poised on the crumbling edge of that great nothingness the Princess hung, hungering with her eyes and straining her fainting ears against the awful splendor of the sky.

Out from the slime and shadows groped the King, thundering: "Back—don't be a fool!"

But down through the thin ether thrilled the still and throbbing warmth of heaven's sun whispering "Leap!"

And the Princess leapt.

43

The Three Wise Men

The comet was blazing down from the sky on the midnight before Christmas. Three songs were dying away in the East: one from the rich and ornate chapel of the great cathedral on the hills beyond 110th Street—a song of beauty and exquisite finish but coldly and formally sung. Another, a chant from the dim synagogue on the lower East Side—heavy with droning and passionate; the last from West 53d Street—a minor wail of utter melody. The songs had died away and the three priests, looking at the midnight sky, saw the comet at the same moment. The priest in the ornate chapel, gowned in his silken vestments, paused and stared wonderingly at the star; it seemed drawing near to him and guiding him. Almost before he knew it he had thrown a rich fur cloak about himself and was whirling downtown in a taxicab, watching the star with fascinated gaze. The rabbi on the lower East Side no sooner saw that blaze in the heavens than a low cry of joy left his lips and he followed swiftly, boarding a passing Grand Street car and clanging up Broadway; he hung on the footboard to watch unmindful of the gibes at his white beard and Jewish gabardine. The old black preacher of 53d Street, with sad and wrinkled face, looked at the moving star thoughtfully and walked slowly with it. So the three men threaded the maze of the Christmas-mad streets, neither looking on the surging crowds nor listening to the shouts of the people, but seeing only the star. The "honk, honk" of the priest's taxicab warned the black priest scarcely too soon, and he staggered with difficulty aside as it whizzed by and made the motorman of the car, which bore the Jew, swear at the carelessness of the chauffeur. One flew, the other whirred swiftly and the third walked slowly; yet because of their differing ways they all came to the steps of the great apartment house at the same moment, and they bowed gravely to each other, yet not without curiosity, as each ascended the steps. The porter was strangely deferential and they rose swiftly to the seventh floor, where a wide hall door flew silently open.

Within and before the wide log fire of the drawing room sat a woman. She was tall and shapely and well gowned. She sat alone. The guests had gone an hour since and the last footsteps of the servants were echoing above; yet she sat there weary, still gazing into the mystery of the fire. She had seen many Christmas Eves and they were growing all to be alike—wretchedly alike. All equally lonely, aimless—almost artificial. She arose once and walked to the window, sweeping aside the heavy curtains, and the brilliancy of the star blazed in upon her. She looked upon it with a start. She remembered how once long, long years ago she had looked upon stars and such things as very real and shining fingers of fate. She remembered especially on a night

---

From *The Crisis* 7 (December 1913): 80–82.

like this how some such star had told her future. How out of her soul wonderful things were to be born, and she had said unto the star: "How shall this be?" And something had answered: "That holy thing that shall be born of you shall be called the Son of God." And then she had cried in all her maiden faith and mystery: "Behold the handmaiden of the Lord, be it according to thy word." And the angel departed from her, and it never came back again. Here she was reaching the portals of middle age with no prospects and few ambitions; to live and wait and sleep; to work a soulless work, to eat in some great manger like this—that was the life that seemed stretching before her endless and without change, until the End and the Change of Changing. And yet she had dreamed such dreams and fancied such fair destiny! As she thought of these dreams to-night a tear gathered and wandered down her face. It was then that she became suddenly aware of two men standing on either side of her, and she felt, but did not see, a third man, who stood behind. But for the soft voice of the first speaker she would have sprung up in alarm, but he was an old man and deferential with soft ascetic Jewish face, with white-forked beard and gabardine, and he bowed in deep humility as he spoke, saying:

"Where is He that is born King of the Jews, for we have seen His star in the East, and have come to worship him?"

The other surpliced figure, who stood upon her right hand, said the same thing, only less:

"Where is He who is born King, for we have seen His star in the East, and have come to worship Him?" And scarcely had his voice ceased than the strong low rolling of another voice came from behind, saying:

"Where is He, for we have seen His star in the East, and have come to worship Him?"

She sank back in her chair and smiled. There was evidently some mistake, and she said to the Jew courteously:

"There is no King here."

"But," said the Jew, eagerly, tremulously, "it is a child we seek, and the star has guided us hither; we have brought gifts of gold and frankincense and myrrh." Still the woman shook her head.

"Children are not allowed in these apartments," she said, "and besides, I am unwed."

The face of the Jew grew radiant.

"The Scriptures say He shall be born of a Virgin," he chanted. But the woman smiled bitterly.

"The children of Virgins are not welcome in the twentieth century, even though they be Sons of God!"

"And in a manger," continued the Jew.

"This is, indeed, a manger," laughed the woman, "but He is not here—He is not here—only—cattle feed here."

Then the silk-robed priest on the left interrupted:

"You do not understand," he said, "it is not a child of the body we seek, but of the Word. The Word which was with God and the Word which was God. We seek the illuminating truth which shall settle all our wild gropings and bring light to this blind world." But the woman laughed even more bitterly.

"I was foolish enough once to think," she said, "that out of my brain would leap some wondrous illuminating word which should give light and warmth to the world, but nothing has been born, save here and there an epigram and the smartness of a phrase. No, He is not here."

The surpliced priest drew back with disappointed mien, and then suddenly, in the face of priest and Jew, as they turned toward the unseen figure at her back, she saw the birth of new and wonderful comprehension—Jew and Gentile sank to their knees—and she heard a soft and mighty voice that came up out of the shadows behind her as she bent forward, almost crouching, and it said:

"Him whom we seek is child neither of thy body nor of thy brain, but of thy heart. Strong Son of God, immortal love. We seek not the king of the world nor the light of the world, but the love of the world, and of all men, for all men; and lo! this thou bearest beneath thy heart, O woman of mankind. This night it shall be born!"

Slowly her heart rose and surged within her as she struggled to her feet; a wonderful revelation lighted in her whirling brain. She, of all women; she, the chosen one—the bride of Almighty God; her lips babbled noiselessly searching for that old and saintly hymn: "My soul doth magnify the Lord, and my spirit hath rejoiced in God, my saviour. For he hath regarded the low estate of his hand-maiden, for behold! from henceforth all generations shall call me blessed." A great new strength gripped her limbs. Slowly she arose, and as she rose, the roof rose silently with her—the walls of the vast room widened—the cold wet pavement touched her satined feet, and the pale-blue brilliance of the star rained on her coiled hair and naked shoulders. The shouting, careless, noisy midnight crowds surged by and brushed her gown. Slowly she turned herself, with strange new gladness in her heart, and the last words of the hymn on her lips: "He hath put down the Mighty from their seats and hath exalted them of low degree; he hath filled the hungry with good things and the rich he hath sent empty away." She turned, and lo! before her stood that third figure, an old, bent black man, sad faced and pitiful, and yet with brilliant caverned eyes and mighty wings that curved to Heaven. And suddenly there was with the angel a multitude of the heavenly hosts praising God and saying:

"Glory to God in the highest; and on earth peace, good will toward men."

SELAH!

44

The Story of Africa

Once upon a time there lay a land in the southern seas; a dark, grim land, walled well against the world. And in that land rose three rivers and a fourth, all flowing out to seek the sea. One river was born amid the Lakes and Mountains of the Moon, sun-kissed, snow-capped, and fled to the northward silent, swiftly; it clambered over the hills and swam the marshes. It threaded the sands—the narrow, choking sands that grew hotter and narrower as it went; yet the river swept on to wider, greener fields, to a laughing plain until through many mouths it burst like a rocket to the Middle Sea with all its myriads of men.

In the wake of the river came dark men creeping, dancing, marching, building, until their pyramids and temples dotted the land and dared the Heavens, and the Thought of their souls and cities was the Beginning of the World.

Far, far away to westward another river leapt and sang and lightly turned its back upon the Sea, rushing to northward. But the grim desert shrieked in its fastnesses crying "Not here!" So the river whirled southward till the black forests cried in their gloom, "Not here!" The river bowed and circled westward. Sullenly, silently, yet proudly, she swept into the western sea. As she swept she sang low minor melody; as she sang she scattered gold carelessly to the black children. But ere she died in the depth of the sea she gave to her strongest and blackest sons, Iron—the precious gift of Iron. They fashioned it cunningly and welded it in faery forms and sent it to the ends of earth to make all men awake. And men awoke. They awoke on the cunning breast of the river's self and kingdom on kingdom arose until the empire of the Songhay rivaled the empires of the world. The sound of the might of Negro land echoed in Carthage and grew in Numibia and gave fairy tales to the Middle Sea.

Away to the south and eastward and below the Mountains of the Moon the third broad river heard her sisters hurrying seaward. North and westward they had gone but she turned to the eternal east. Golden she lifted up her golden hands and stretched to Ophir, Punt and Tarshish her long, lithe finger. Her voice rose mighty in song until with a million stars in her throat she dropped wild singing in the southern sea and shuddered to the vastness of its silence.

Her black children sat in mine, fortress, temple and flowering field and traded with dark traders beyond the India Sea, till lo: out of the north came a cry, a cry like the anguish of a soul. For back in the bowels of the land men heard the running of three rivers and rushed away madly; for they were those that would not hear and could not see. On they ran, on, on and eastward ringing their spears and crying their great, awful cry of war. As locusts swarming they passed the north of the glooming

From *The Crisis* 8 (September 1914): 234–235.

forest with its dim red faerie; eastward they looked upon the inland oceans and southward they sent their war cry reeling to the Mountains of the Moon.

There came a shouting in the wilderness and again as swarming bees onward they came, and again the war cry echoed to the stars. Over the ruin of things that were passed that black and human flood until its angry surf dashed to into the vast, red Heart of the Land, and knew the haunted spell-cursed realm of Last River. Mighty was this last of rivers—a river of rivers, an endless lacing and swirling and curling and swelling and streaming of wild, weird waters beneath the giant jungle, where the lion, the leopard and the elephant slept with the long, slim snake.

Hand in hand and voice to voice these waters whirled in one vast circle within the bosom of the land saying their incantations. They shouldered past the mountains and sang past all the seas, then shunning the glaring desert and in-gathering themselves to one swarming flood they thrilled and thundered on the sea. Snake-like and lion strong they gathered the children, the little dark and weeping children, and lo, beyond on swelling waters rose a hoarse, harsh cry and slim and sail-like fingers beckoned to the westward deeps. The river paused and rose red and reeking in the sunlight—thundered to the sea—thundered through the sea in one long line of blood, with tossing limbs and the echoing cries of death and pain.

On, on! the bloody waters, with those pale ghost fingers of ship and sail, with gold and iron, hurt and hell, rolled, swelled and tumbled, until the laughing islands of the western sea grew dark and dumb with pain and in the world, the great new world, a Sorrow was planted and the Sorrow grew.

45

Of the Children of Peace

Come, all my father's children, and sit beside my knee, here with this child of mine, and listen:

Have you ever seen a soldier? It is a brave sight, is it not? Once upon a time, many, many years before your dear little curly heads were born, I remember seeing an army that marched because a King was visiting an Emperor. Berlin was joy mad. Houses streamed with color and music reeled and rioted. Then came the army. Tall, handsome men, all gold and silver and broadcloth, sworded, spurred and plumed, led on horses that curvetted and tossed their shining bits. (Do you not love a horse with his great, sweet eyes and quivery shining softness?) Next came the soldiers, erect, rigid, "Eyes left!" Pit-pat, pit-pat! Clasping their little innocent guns. Next came the artillery: files of wildly prancing horses dragging long leaden things. How the crowd roared. The King bowed to the Emperor and the Emperor bowed to the King, and there rose a great cry of pride and joy and battle from the people. With that cry I seemed suddenly to awake. I somehow saw *through;* (you know sometimes how you seem to see, but are blind until something happens and you really see?)

I saw then what I see now. I saw and see the WAR that men said could not be.

Gone was all the brave tinsel, the glitter, sheen and music. The men trudged and limped, naked and dirty, with sodden, angry, distorted faces; their eyes were sunken and bloodshot, with murder in them; they staggered over corpses and severed arms and feet and dead horses and they carried—not little innocent guns, but little innocent children; they dragged, not pale and leaden guns, but pale and bounden women, and before them staggered and crept old women and grandfathers, the sick and the maimed, the weak and the half-grown boys and girls.

I heard the cry that hovered over this fearsome army: it was a wail of hunger and crime, of thirst and pain and death, and the cry rose and met an answering cry that came from beyond the forest to the West.

Two toddling children slipped from their fathers' arms and met in the gloom of that forest, where the beasts cowered and livid, disbodied hands seemed to creep in the darkness.

"Mother," they whispered.

"Mama," they cried.

"Mütterchen," they sobbed.

Wild with horror two bound mothers beat their naked hands against the gun-carriages, groping and struggling through the gloom, as death flamed through their hearts.

Then the armies met. Two fathers leapt from the two armies ahead and each

---

From *The Crisis* 8 (October 1914): 289–290.

seized the other's child. They strangled and crushed and maimed and murdered it, till each baby lay pale, limp and dead.

(Nay, shrink not, my children; horrible as the tale may be, the truth is worse and you must know it.)

Then War was loose. Then six million human beings left their fields of golden grain and the busy hum of their factories and taking their own children for weapons dashed them against the trees and the lampposts and the churches and wallowed and gasped in their blood!

Come, all my father's children and hear how beyond the blue mists of the Everlasting Sea, the mothers mad with hunger, grief and pain, are fronting the blood-stained heavens with bared and haunted breasts and are shrieking:

"Why?"

"Why?"

Their shriek is the booming of guns, and the booming of cannon is the shriek of mothers.

And you must answer, Children of Peace, you must answer!

You must cry: "There is no why!"

"The cause of War is Preparation for War."

"The cause of Preparation for War is the Hatred and Despising of Men, your and my Brothers."

"War is murder in a red coat."

"War is raped mothers and bleeding fathers and strangled children."

"War is Death, Hate, Hunger and Pain!"

"Hell is War!"

And when you believe this with all your little hearts;

And when you cry it across the seas and across the years with all your little voices—

Then shall the mothers of all dead children hear;

Then shall the Sisters of all dead Brothers hear; then shall the Daughters of all dead Fathers hear; then shall the Women rise and say:

"War is done."

"Henceforward and forever there shall be no organized murder of men, for the children we bear shall be the Children of Peace, else there shall be no children."

Amen!

But cry, little children, cry and cry loud and soon, for until you and the Mothers speak, the men of the world bend stupid and crazed beneath the burden of hate and death. Behold, this old and awful world is but one slaughter-pen, one tale of innocent blood and senseless hate and strife.

Look yonder! In the gloomy forest all is still, save here a red and flickering flame and there a last trembling sob. Only one living thing passes across the night: a horse—a gaunt, sweating horse, with bloody nostrils, great pain-struck eyes, and bowels trailing on the earth. He hears his Emperor bugling "Victory!" to the King. Turning he staggers toward him and whimpers as he goes.

46

The Second Coming

Three bishops sat in San Francisco, New Orleans and New York, peering gloomily into three flickering fires which cast and recast shuddering shadows on book-lined walls. Three letters lay in their laps and said:

"And thou, Valdosta, in the land of Georgia, art not least among the princes of America, for out of thee shall come a Governor who shall rule my people."

The white Bishop of New York scowled and impatiently threw the paper into the fire.

"Valdosta?" he said, "that's where I go to the Governor's wedding of little Marguerite, my white flower—" Then he forgot the writing in his musing, but the paper flared red in the fireplace.

"Valdosta?" said the black bishop in New Orleans, and turned uneasily in his chair. "I must go down there. Those colored folk are acting strangely. I don't know where all this unrest and moving will lead to. Then, there's poor Lucy—" And he threw the letter into the fire; but eyed it suspiciously, as it flamed green.

"Stranger things than that have happened," he said slowly, "and ye shall hear of wars and rumors of wars . . . for nation shall rise against nation and kingdom against kingdom."

In San Francisco the priest of Japan, abroad to study strange lands, sat in his lacquer chair with face like soft yellow and wrinkled parchment. Slowly he wrote in a great and golden book:

"I have been strangely bidden to the Vale of Dosta where one of those religious cults that swarm here will welcome a Prophet. I shall go and report to Kioto."

So, in the dim waning of the day before Christmas, three bishops met in Valdosta and saw its mills and storehouses, its wide-throated and sandy streets in the mellow glow of a crimson sun. The governor glared anxiously up the street as he helped the Bishop of New York into his car and welcomed him graciously.

"I am troubled," he said, "about the Niggers. They are acting queer. I'm not certain but Fleming is back of it."

"Fleming?"

"Yes; he's running against me next term for governor; he's a fire-brand; wants niggers to vote and all that—Pardon me a moment, there's a darky I know—" and he hurried to the black bishop, who had just descended from the "Jim Crow" car, and clasped his hand cordially. They talked in whispers.

"Search diligently," said the governor in parting, "and bring me word again." Then returning to his Guest: "You will excuse me, won't you?" he said, "but I am sorely troubled. I never saw niggers act so. They're leaving by the hundreds and those

---

From *The Crisis* 15 (December 1917): 59–60.

who stay are getting impudent. They seem to be expecting something. What's the crowd, Jim?"

The chauffeur said that there was some sort of Chinese official in town and everybody wanted to glimpse him. He drove around another way.

It all happened very suddenly. The Bishop of New York, in full canonicals for the early wedding, stepped out on the rear balcony of his mansion, just as the dying sun lit crimson clouds of glory in the East and burned the West.

"Fire!" yelled a wag in the surging crowd that was gathering to celebrate a southern Christmas Eve; all laughed and ran.

The bishop did not understand. He peered around. Was it that dark little house in the far back yard that flamed? Forgetful of his robes, he hurried down—a brave white figure in the sunset. He found himself before an old black rickety stable. He could hear the mules stamping within.

No, it was not fire. It was the sunset glowing through the cracks. Behind the hut its glory rose toward God like flaming wings of Cherubim. He paused until he heard the faint wail of a child. Hastily he entered. A white girl crouched before him, down by the very mules' feet, with a baby in her arms. A little mite of a baby that wailed weakly. Behind mother and child stood a shadow. The bishop turned to the right, inquiringly, and saw a black man in bishop's robes that faintly echoed his own. Hastily he turned away to the left and saw a golden Japanese in golden garb. Then he heard the black man mutter behind him:

"But He was to come the second time in clouds of glory, with the nations gathered around Him and angels—" at the word a shaft of glorious light fell full upon the child, while without came the tramping of unnumbered feet and the whirring of winds.

The Bishop of New York bent quickly above the baby.

It was black!

The bishop stepped back with a gesture of disgust, hardly listening to and yet hearing the black bishop who spoke almost as if in apology:

"She ain't really white; I know Lucy—you see, her mother worked for the Governor—" The bishop turned on his heel and nearly trod on the yellow priest, who knelt with bowed head before the pale mother and offered incense and a gift of gold.

Out into the night rushed the bishop. The wings of the Cherubim were folded back against the stars. As he hastened down the front stair-case the governor came rushing up the street steps.

'We are late," he cried nervously. "The Bride awaits." He hurried the bishop to the waiting limousine, asking him anxiously:

"Did you hear anything? Do you hear that noise? The crowd is growing strangely on the streets and there seems to be a fire over toward the East. I never saw so many people here—I fear violence—a mob—a lynching—hark!" What was that which the Bishop, too, heard beneath the rhythm of unnumbered feet? Deep in his heart a wonder grew. What was it? Ah, he knew. It was music—some strong and mighty chord. It rose higher as the brilliantly-lighted church split the night and swept radiantly toward them. The governor, ashen-faced, crouched in the car; but the bishop said softly as the ecstacy pulsed in his heart:

"Such music, such wedding music! What choir is it?"

47

The Flight into Egypt

You remember, do you not?—the beautiful Bible story in the simple words of Matthew, telling of the departure of the Three Wise Men:

> "And when they were departed, behold, the angel of the Lord appeareth to Joseph in a dream, saying, Arise, and take the young child and his mother, and flee into Egypt, and be thou there until I bring thee word: for Herod will seek the young child and destroy him.
>
> "When he arose, he took the young child and his mother by night, and departed into Egypt:
>
> "And was there until the death of Herod: that it might be fulfilled which was spoken of the Lord by the prophet, saying, Out of Egypt have I called my son."

They were poor, humble, ignorant people,—albeit the blood of kings burned in their veins. They were ragged and unkempt and black. Long years they had plodded faithfully to earn their daily bread in sweat and pain; then one night, beneath the stars, came Three Strangers, crying: "Where is He that is Born?" The mother lifted Him up tenderly and they gave him gifts.—Candy and a Fairy-tale and a piece of Gold.

Joseph and Mary looked at the gold-piece in amazement. Never had they seen so much money before, and as they looked they dreamed. Egypt! the Land of Freedom; Egypt! the Haven of the Oppressed; Egypt! where there was Learning and Wages and Honor. While here? Here there brooded a Shadow and a Fear.

Stealthily they arose by night and took the old lantern and walked and ran till they crossed the river. The dawn found them wet and weary, crouching in the moss-swept underbrush of the swamp; but their faces were set North—that it might be fulfilled which was spoken of the Lord by the prophet—that the fairy-tale might come true.

From *The Crisis* 17 (December 1918): 59.

48

Steve

He was a lank puppy when he came—long, and dull gold on his crinkly hair, furtive and frightened, but his eyes were the eyes of the Crucified Christ. The Girl took him in and plead for him—fed him when she thought of it and overfed him after she forgot. He was wild with the joy of a home and bounded in shooting leaps across the meadows. The Woman, who was wiser than we and knew that dogs are more than human, looked on him coldly at first, for she had loved dogs before, and love is a terrible thing.

Once he was lost and I and the Girl sought him as the sun died in the west, sought him east and west and north—calling and whistling—till at last he came darting like an arrow out of the unknown dark to leap and fawn upon us and bark triumphantly. Once he was stolen, but after two nights he crept back to us, dirty and bedraggled, with the accusing rope tied around him. Ah! but we were glad, and to celebrate we bought a collar and set his name brightly upon it.

Then of a certain Sunday morning catastrophe threatened us—two Russians stood without the gate and said, "It is our dog," and "Larrabee!" they called and he went, wagging his tail. But the Woman came quietly to the door and said, "Steve!" and he leapt back in joy and wriggled on her and kissed her. Then there was parleying and tales of his beautiful wolf-hound mother and—"But will you take him?" asked the Woman, her voice soft with fear. The Russian wife patted him tenderly and said, "No, we go back to Russia, now that Revolution has brought Freedom, and leave him with you, for he loves you and you are kind." So then the Girl left her hiding and her tears and clasped her treasure, and the Russians went back—Great God! to what?

And the dog waxed strong and mighty, golden and beautiful. Men feared his very sight, and his seldom bark was a forest of sound; but he loved the Woman with an endless love—following her every footstep, harkening to her every word, guarding her every movement. The Girl he liked next; and me he tolerated good-naturedly. To our guests he was studiously polite, with the grave courtesy of the greatly born; to all children he was humble servant—but the Woman was God!

Then came the end. After two years of delights, after the wonder of a new home, after a summer by the sounding sea and winters in snows; after great dreamful naps and terrifying forays; after evenings of strange, weird music—after all this came slow steps and pain and the great frightened look of love in his eyes grew more and more wistful as he followed the Woman whither his palsied legs could not go. So they came and took him away and gave him strange medicine to eat, but the light died in his eyes and in mercy they put him to sleep. The Woman wept.

He is gone. Last night, meseems, he slept beside the werewolves who guard the

---

From *The Crisis* 17 (December 1918): 62–63.

angels of the throne of God. At dawn I saw his soul flashing in golden flame across the northern skies; and now at noon behold him, leaping with mighty bounds across the broad steppes of his fathers. I hear his great voice sounding above the chaos of the beautifulest dream of two centuries, when the Christ of the Bolsheviki cried in God-begotten faith to the boiling, angry, fear-mad waters, "Peace!" and there was no peace. I feel his golden fleece bristling with almighty curses and his fangs dripping blood above the Huns who would destroy, not alone the flesh, but the spirit of a great people. On, Steve, on! rend and tear and kill and die that the sweet, good earth may live again and that Russia may not die.

All this I see (for I am Seer), but in our deserted home the Girl is silent and the Woman weeps, while I? Oh, I, always, beneath the hand of fate, write—and write—and write.

49

The Gospel According to Mary Brown

She was very small and pretty and black and lived in the cabin beyond the Big Road and down the lane by the creek, there where field on field of green cotton was flowering in the spring. And one night as she sat there all alone and wistful, watching the stars, a woman passed by and hailed her. She shrank back in the shadows, but the woman smiled and said full softly:

"Fear not, Mary: for thou hast found favor with God."

And then Mary knew, and she brought out the Old Book and read the lines aloud, following them with her little dark finger:

"My soul doth—magnify the Lord. . . .

"For He hath regarded the low—estate of his handmaiden, for behold from—henceforth all—generations shall call me blessed . . ."

Even as she read the door flew wide, and Pain stood beside her. He thrust and threw her poor little body and wracked and burst her thews in sunder. She moaned, but did not scream—and thus at last, in years of hours, she brought forth her first-born son; and she called his name Joshua.

Day after day she sat and watched his perfect little form. Was he not a beautiful baby? His skin was black velvet; his eyes were star-sown midnights, set in milk; his tiny teeth, white pearls; and his hair all tender tendrils of silk.

Sometimes—some very little times—a pain caught her as she cuddled him close. Would it not be better for him if he were whiter? Brown, or yellow, or dusky cream? Then she would say fiercely: No! No! Is not Love, who is God, his Father? And would his Father send a black baby to this world just to make him suffer?

And so each night after work she took him out beneath the stars, and the glory of the Lord shone round about them, and she heard the angels singing:

"Glory to God in the highest and on earth Peace, good-will toward men."

Thus did Mary, the mother, begin to dream dreams. And the child grew and waxed strong in spirit, filled with wisdom, and the grace of God was upon him.

Now his mother went to town every Christmas to settle for her crops, but it was not until he was twelve years old that he went with her, and saw town for the first. How marvelous and wonderful to him was the revelation.

Mary finished her work and started home, but Joshua tarried behind. When Mary found him not, she turned back seeking him. After three days she found him in a church, sitting in the midst of the deacons, both hearing them and asking them questions:

From *The Crisis* 19 (December 1919): 41–43.

Why were colored folk poor?
Why were they afraid?
Whose father was God?
Did the deacons know God? Well, he did. God was his own Father.
And all that heard him were astonished at his understanding and answers. But his mother said unto him:
"Son, why did you do me this-a-way?"
And he answered: "Wist ye not, that I must be about my Father's business."
And Mary caught her breast in pain, for how may a father be mentioned when one's father is only God? But she kept all his sayings in her heart.

So Joshua went back to the plantation and worked. He ploughed and picked cotton and hoed and drove mules and, finally, learned to be a carpenter; and always he increased in wisdom and stature and in favor with God and man.

But not, alas! with all white men. Most of them mistrusted him. They could not place him. He was neither sullen nor impudent. But he looked at them with a certain, clear understanding and calm sense of authority; he carried himself like a man, and this they resented.

"Is not this the carpenter, the son of Mary?" they asked. "Didn't we keep him on the plantation and out of school? And yet, he's strutting and talking and preaching; he's putting ideas into niggers' heads." And they slipped down to the old wooden church by the creek and listened to him preach.

The people were scattered on the green under the trees, eating their lunch out of baskets. And Joshua opened his mouth and taught them, saying:

"Blessed are the poor; blessed are they that mourn; blessed are the meek; blessed are the merciful; blessed are they which are persecuted. All men are brothers and God is the Father of all."

Then all the multitude lifted up their voices and sang: "Good news, the Chariot's a comin'."

"What kind of talk is this?" said the White Folk, "Behold, he stirreth up the people."

Whereupon they took council together. They stopped his preaching and doubled his work. They cursed and drove his hearers; they warned and beat them.

Mary watched all this in mounting terror. She saw the hurt in Joshua's eyes and the bitterness in his heart. She knew that he suffered, not simply in himself, but with every other sufferer. That he was wounded by every sin and bruised by every injustice. He was oppressed and he was afflicted, yet he opened not his mouth. She saw him walk daily, despised and rejected of men, a man of sorrows and acquainted with grief. The world hid its face from him and esteemed him not.

Bitter, ever more bitter, grew the White Folk at his silent protest—his humble submission to wrong. They seized him and questioned him.

"What do you mean by this talk about all being brothers—do you mean social equality?"

"What do you mean by 'the meek shall inherit the earth'—do you mean that niggers will own our cotton land?"

"What do you mean by saying God is you-all's father—is God a nigger?"

And Joshua flamed in mighty anger and answered and said: "Woe unto you, Scribes and Pharisees, hypocrites! Fill ye up then the measure of your fathers. Ye serpents, ye generation of vipers, how can ye escape the damnation of hell!"

In wild fury the mob seized him and haled him before a judge.

The Judge—he was from the North—was sorely puzzled. "What shall I do with him?" he asked helplessly.

"Kill the nigger," yelled the mob.

"Why, what evil hath he done?"

But they cried out the more, saying: "Let him be crucified."

Thereupon the Judge washed his hands of the whole matter, saying: "I am innocent of his blood."

And so swiftly he was sentenced for treason and inciting murder and insurrection; quickly they hurried him to the jail-yard, where they stripped him, and spit upon him, and smote him on the head, and mocked, and lynched him. And sitting down, they watched him die.

And Joshua said: "Father, forgive them, for they know not what they do."

Now far down in the cabin beyond the Big Road and down the lane by the creek, there where field on field on bronze-stalked cotton lay bursting in white clouds, awaiting the pickers, a mother strove with heaven, on her knees. And she cried!

"God, you ain't fair—You ain't fair, God! You didn't ought to do it—if you didn't want him black, you didn't have to make him black; if you didn't want him unhappy, why did you let him think? And then you let them mock him, and hurt him, and lynch him! Why, why did you do it God?"

And then afar she heard the faint pit-a-pat of running feet; she paused on her knees. Pit-a-pat they came across the field, down the Big Road, along the lane; pit-a-pat-pit-a-pat; and then she heard the hard breathing—ha-ha! Ha-ha!—Pit-a-pat—pit-a-pat, until suddenly a flying sweat-swarthed figure rushed on her, crying: "Mary—Mary—he is not dead: He is risen!"

He came in the twilight, walking slowly, with head thrust slightly forward, as was his wont, and eyes upon the ground. But the heart of Mary leapt within her. For his hair shone, the lines were gone from his face, and the sorrow slept in his eyes. His clothes were white and whole and clean, and his voice was the voice of God.

And Mary said: "Where was you, Son?"

And he answered and said: "I was crucified, dead, and buried. I descended into Hell. On the third day I rose from the dead. I ascended into Heaven, and sit on the right hand of my Father, from whence I shall come to judge the Quick and the Dead."

And softly Mary laid herself down at His feet, and died.

50

Again, Social Equality

Mr. Paleface entered his parlor mincingly,—"My dear man," he said, expressively.

"I am Brownson," said the dark man quietly.

"Of course—of course—I know you well, and your people. My father was an abolitionist, and I had a black mammy—"

Mr. Brownson looked out of the window, and said rapidly:

"I have come to ask for certain rights and privileges. My people—"

"—suffer; I know it; I know it. I have often remarked what a shame it was. Sir, it is an outrage!"

"—yes; we want to ask—"

Mr. Paleface raised a deprecating finger, "Not social equality," he murmured,—"I trust you are not asking that."

"Certainly not," said Brownson. "I think the right of a man to select his friends and guests and decide with whom he will commit matrimony, is sacredly his and his alone."

"Good—good! Now, my man, we can talk openly, face to face. We can pour out our souls to each other. What can I do? I have already sent my annual check to Hampton."

"Sir, we want to vote."

"Ah! That is difficult—difficult. You see, voting has come to have a new significance. We used to confine our votes to politics, but now—bless me!—we are voting religion, work, social-reform, landscape-gardening, and art. Then, too, women are in politics—you see—well, I'm sure you sense the difficulties. Moreover, what is voting? A mere form—the making and execution of laws is the thing, and there I promise you that I—"

"Well, then; we would help in carrying out the laws."

"Commendable ambition. Very, very commendable. But this involves even greater difficulties. Administrators and executives are thrown closely together—often in the same room—at the same desk. They have to mingle and consult. Much as I deplore the fact, it is true, that a man will not sit at a desk or work at a bench with a man whose company at a theatre he would resent."

"I see," said Brownson, thoughtfully. "I presume, then, it is our business to demand this right to sit in theatres and places of popular entertainment."

"Good Lord, man, that's impossible! Civil rights like this cannot be forced. Objectionable persons must grow, develop—er wash, before—"

From *The Crisis* 19 (March 1920): 236–237.

"Then I am sure you will help me clean and train my people. I want to join in the great movements for social uplift."

"Splendid! I will have some movements organized for your folks."

"No, I want to be part of the general movement, so as to get the training and inspiration, the wide outlook—the best plans."

"Are you crazy? Don' you know that social uplift work consists of a series of luncheons, dinners, and teas, with ladies present?"

"Um," said Brownson. "I see. I, also, see that in answering your first question, I made a mistake. In the light of your subsequent definition, I see that social equality, far from being what I don't want, is precisely what I do want."

'I knew it!" screamed Mr. Paleface. "I knew it all the time; I saw it sneaking into your eyes. You want—you dare to want to marry my sister."

"Not if she looks like you," said Brownson, "and not if she's as big a liar."

"Get out—get out—leave my house you ungrateful—"

51

Of Giving Work

"We give you people work and if we didn't, how would you live?"

The speaker was a southern white man. He was of the genus called "good." He had come down from the Big House to advise these Negroes, in the forlorn little church which crouched on the creek. He didn't come to learn, but to teach. The result was that he did not learn, and he saw only that blank, impervious gaze which colored people know how to assume; and that dark wall of absolute silence which they have a habit of putting up instead of applause. He felt awkward, but he repeated what he had said, because he could not think of anything else to say:

"We give you people work, and if we didn't, how would you live?"

And then the old and rather ragged black man arose in the back of the church and came slowly forward and as he came, he said:

"And we gives you homes; and we gives you cotton; and we makes your land worth money; and we waits on you and gets your meals and cleans up your dirt. And if we didn't, do all those things for you, how would you live?"

The white man choked and got red, but the old black man went on talking:

"And what's more: we gives you a heap more than you gives us and we's getting mighty tired of the bargain—"

"I think we ought to give you fair wages," stammered the white man.

"And that ain't all," continued the old black man, "we ought to have something to say about your wages. Because if what *you* gives us gives *you* a right to say what we ought to get, then what *we* gives you gives *us* a right to say what *you* ought to get; and we're going to take that right *some day*."

The white man blustered:

"That's Bolshevism!" he shouted.

And the church broke up.

52

Clothes

It was in a Southern city and the white people were on the one and favorite subject—the "Nig-ra". This time it was health, a safe and absorbing subject. They were told of the horrible danger of having their clothes washed in Negro cabins and of their consequent personal interest in the Negroes' health.

There ensued that succession of little purrs and squeals which some ladies consider evidence of the highest breeding.

But one Southern white woman rose and said calmly, "Yes, there is danger, but there's more danger to the Negroes in your dirty clothes than to you from the clean and sterilized washing which they return."

Then followed the eloquent silence that does not need words.

From *The Crisis* 20 (August 1920): 166.

53

Pontius Pilate

Pontius Pilate, Federal Governor of Mississippi, sat in the Judgment seat at Jackson. Before him stretched a table of shining gold and the morning sun sang through the eastern windows. It lighted the faces of the Chief Priest and the Elders as they bent eagerly toward him, and twisted itching hands.

He was fingering a pile of silver money which seemed to have been tossed or thrown upon the table before him.

"This-er-Iscariot fellow," he began in a low, inquiring voice, while his eyes sought the haunting shadows of the long, crimson curtains at his back.

A bishop interrupted him: a tall and mighty bishop cassocked, ringed, and jewelled:

"Just a case of uneasy conscience—a worthless fellow—we shall give this to foreign missions, shall we not, and seek Souls for the Kingdom?" And he gathered up and counted out thirty pieces—"and now to the main matter."

"I don't see how I can pardon this Barabbas," said the Governor,—speaking with sudden vehemence. "He is a criminal and a drunkard—he has killed men before and—"

"Now, now, Governor!" interrupted the Judge, "Jack Barabbas is not so bad—quarrelsome, to be sure, when in liquor, and quick to defend his honor as every white man should be. Moreover—hark!"

Something floated in by the window. It was a low, but monstrous sound and in it lay anger and blood.

"See, Governor? Hear that? The Saturday crowds are in town and Jack is a prime favorite—you know they're none too well disposed toward you and the Government since this new usurpation of federal power."

"That's just it," answered the Governor angrily, straightening in his chair and flashing challenging glances right and left: "Lawlessness has brought Mississippi to this pass and yet you want me not ony to pardon a notorious criminal, but also to condemn an innocent man."

"Innocent?" cried several voices, but the great voice of the Bishop outdrowned them all.

"You do not understand," he said ominously, thrusting forward his great bulk and towering over the nervous frame of the Governor. The Governor stiffened but did not quail. "You are northern born—you live far from our problem—our fearful Problem. Remember, Sir, in Mississippi there is one Crime of Crimes, one beside which all crimes fade to innocence—Murder, Arson, Rape, Theft—all are nothing beside the crime of Race Equality. Sir, this man, whom we have brought before you,

---

From *The Crisis* 21 (December 1920): 53–54.

not only preaches openly the equality of all men, but (and the Bishop shuddered) *practices it!"*

And then the flying words of all the eager, angry councilors raised and swept across the golden board and up the crimson curtains and down the open, sun-flushed windows:

'Do you know what he wants?"—"He wants equality for Everybody—everybody, mind you"—"Turks, Jews, Niggers, Dagoes, Chinks, Japs"—"everybody"—"talking, sleeping, kissing, marrying"—"the damned scoundrel!"—"and do you know why he wants it?"—"He's nothing but a—"—"He's a Bolshevist—a Red Revolutionist"—"He is going to overthrow all government—"

And then in a shriek—"He claims to be God and King."

Slowly, Pilate arose.

"Bring him in," he said.

They swung the crimson curtains back and there in the shadows stood the Christ. Pontius Pilate shuddered. "Art thou King?" he whispered.

And the answer came calm and clear, "Yes!"

The cry of the mob below shivered to a shriek, while the Chief Priest and the Elders stood in a silence that was ominous.

Pilate turned.

"I find no fault in this man," he said doggedly, as his hands trembled.

"He blasphemed against the White Race," hissed the Bishop.

But Pilate continued: "You have brought this man before me as a dangerous agitator. I have examined him before you and have found no fault in him. I will therefore fine him and let him go."

But the council cried in one voice.

"Away with Christ—and pardon Barabbas!"

"I'll pardon Barabbas if you insist—but Christ—"

Again the groan of the mob rose and flooded in at the window, breaking the sunshine.

Pilate stirred uneasily—"I won't punish him," he said testily. "I know no law."

"Sir, we know our unwritten law. The crowd below—"

"I'll have no violence," cried Pilate. "It was just this lynching business that led the federal government to interfere in Mississippi—"

"Your Excellency, consider a moment," interrupted the States Attorney. "You incur no responsibility. You simply deliver this man into our hands; and by your pardon of Barabbas the crowd will be mollified and—"

"And what?" asked the Governor.

"Well, there will be less likelihood of violence."

Pilate arose agitated. "I'll have nothing to do with it," he said. "I wash my hands of the whole thing."

The councilors bowed and turned to the door. The shout of the mob rose and rent the courtyard and the sunlight died:

—Lynch him! Lynch the damned—!

For a moment Pilate hesitated with clenched hands and riven face. Then slowly he left the chamber.

It was late afternoon and Pilate stood in the clean, cool bathroom, washing his hands. His wife hurried in.

"Pontius," she said hesitatingly, "have nothing to do with that just man—for I have suffered—"

"There, there! It's all right," he said, chucking her under the chin. "Don't meddle in politics." They both started, for they heard the mad music of myriad feet, the laughter, screaming and cursing of men, and the shrill babble of women's voices; and then over the height of the hills rolled the far-off echo of that world-worn cry:

"My God, my God! Why has Thou forsaken me!'

54

Chamounix

I have seen the League of Nations, the Federation of the World, sitting in a little upper room and stared at by reporters, amidst streams of hopes and fears and of intrigues. After that I came to Chamounix—to cow bells and silence and trickle of waters. Above this world-on-end, lies the vast Thing of Snow,—silent, tremendous, a world a part, remembered and forgotten; a place of lights and shadows, unknown to earth. And of mists. I think the real marriage of earth and stars lies somehow in these mists. There is every preparation for it: the calm and pretty valley with its cows, with its homes, its little intrigues and tragedies, its laughter and flowers. Then gradually and gravely uplifted, the pointing pines; the fingers of the sullen, steadfast pines, pointing, always pointing. And then a space of lichen, leaf and brown gorse; and then a wide grey pause of utter rock, weirdly a waste, grim in its sense of age and strength. After that the snows, the white and blue and golden snows with their feet drabbled in the earth.

What more fitting approach to the stars, to the thoughts that lie beyond the world, enchained and hallowed? One sees this mirage of earth and skies as a mist, a grey and white uncertainty, where line and point drift, merge and dissolve into somthing that is just cloud and sky.

Last night in the rift of the world formed by the serried snow-broidered edge of the Alps, I saw the moon sailing in seas of sounds and tints of tawny green and hurrying waters; without the narrow rift, lifted their heads, snows of clouds and clouds of snows, mountains real and mountains spiritual, clouds of mountains and mountains of clouds, until the world, the great soiled world, was a thing so beautiful, so rare, so still and sweet that life seemed all love and wonder. I could almost hear the sounds of stars raining down upon Mont Blanc: the mist of the rain was moon shine there on the dim White Mountain, and the song of the sound of it was as the voice of death calling to the victorious. It was like white age above the brutal strength of youth; it was sweet childhood which is always apart and beyond the scarred and moaning world. How singular is this ceaseless sound of waters, the dripping and dropping of snows, the roar of fallen mists, the dashing of clouds in the slow, grey and crumpled rivers of riven ice. And yet against the voice of the waters is the voice of the mountain; it is the mountain audible, the song of snows, the color of space, the feeling of things without end. The mountain is unmoveable; day and day, night after night we have flown and whirled about it, changed to city after city and ridden over hill and dale, resting and running, yet the mountain is always there, pale and calm and motionless, curiously eternal.

If I lived here long I should pray to Mont Blanc, throwing my hands in ecstacy,

---

From *The Crisis* 23 (December 1921); 56–58.

screaming my tears. I should heap fire against it and vow gold and jewels. It should be God. For what else can God be but a Mountain or the Sea?

In that transforming miracle of the mountain and the mist there is always sinking to earth some solemn singing as of things and of thoughts that rise above, beyond and athwart the heavy tongued earth and melt to something vaster and truer. It is midnight in the valley. I cannot sleep, for the mountain never sleeps and the moon tonight is widely awake. I sit and scribble and then ever and again creep to my window. The marvel of it, the sheer, inhuman perfectness of it all, the almost pain of its beauty and hurt of its joy! It is there still in the morning. The White Wraith has melted into the sky, throwing earthwards one long pale finger. Its feet are the founding stones of the universe and its head is lost with the stars. Its thoughts are the thoughts of God. The world is grey and black with purple interludes. The waters wail. At last the long shaft dies there from the topmost shoulder of the mighty hill and with its death the mist drops nearer to the black and burning earth. And always the pines point upward.

55

The Sermon in the Cradle

Now when Jesus was born in Benin of Nigeria in the days of English rule, behold, there came wise men from the East to London.

Saying, Where is he that is born King of the Blacks? For we have seen his star in the east, and are come to worship him.

When the Prime Minister had heard these things, he was troubled, and all England with him.

And when he had gathered all the chief priests and scholars of the land together, he demanded of them where this new Christ should be born.

And they said unto him, in Benin of Nigeria: for thus it was written by the prophet:

And thou Benin, in the land of Nigeria, art not the least among the princes of Africa: for out of thee shall come a Governor, that shall rule my Negro people.

Then the Prime Minister, when he had privily called the wise men, inquired of them diligently what time the star appeared.

And he sent them to Benin, and said, "Go and search diligently for the young child; and when ye have found him, bring me word again, that I may come and worship him also."

When they had heard the Premier, they departed; and lo, the star, which they saw in the east, went before them, till it came and stood over where the young child was.

When they saw the star, they rejoiced with exceeding great joy.

And when they were come into the house, they saw the young child with Mary his mother, and fell down, and worshipped him: and when they had opened their treasures, they presented unto him gifts: gold and medicine and perfume.

And being warned of God in a dream that they should not return to England, they departed into their own country another way.

Save one, and he was black. And his own country was the country where he was; so the black Wise Man lingered by the cradle and the new-born babe.

The perfume of his gift rose and filled the house until through it and afar came the dim form of years and multitudes. And the child, seeing the multitudes, opened his mouth and taught them, saying:

Blessed are poor folks for they shall go to heaven.
Blessed are sad folks for someone will bring them joy.
Blessed are they that submit to hurts for they shall sometime own the world.
Blessed are they that want to do right for they shall get their wish.
Blessed are those who do not seek revenge for vengeance will not seek them.

From *The Crisis* 23 (December 1921): 58–59.

Blessed are the pure for they shall see God.
Blessed are those who will will not fight for they are God's children.
Blessed are those whom people like to injure for they shall sometime be happy.
Blessed are you, Black Folk, when men make fun of you and mob you and lie about you. Never mind and be glad for your day will surely come.
Always the world has ridiculed its better souls.

56

The Spanish Fandango

The audience was ideal—small, rapt and responsive. Afterward in the Parish House we danced amid fresh young joy. Then in an upper room at midnight we foregathered: there was Dabney, of course, master without ceremony; and Gilpin with his voice—that wonderful rolling depth of sounding reverberations, shot with laughter. One of us had run for the Legislature last year—another handled autos, etc. We drank ginger-ale that had a reminiscent—slightly suspicious—taste. (Gilpin didn't like it—he said he didn't want the flavor spoiled with ginger-ale!) Then one at the piano played an obligato to our talk and laughter, low enticing things, yet not interrupting. We ate—there were biscuits and tender golden chicken and more— and talked reminiscently. Next Dabney bringing out his banjo rollicked Gilpin dancing to his feet. Dabney told an inimitable story of an Uncle Tom's Cabin Company in old Richmond days, all colored: Eliza came in from the wrong side and met the dogs instead of fleeing from them. The dogs got to fighting—the audience was entranced, convulsed.

Then at last—it was 2 A.M.—Dabney took down the Golden Guitar and all was still. He played softly the Spanish Fandango.

Have you ever heard Dabney play the Spanish Fandango? Dear God!

There will be threads of smoke, and sprawling, indistinct men; a tiny tuning as of drops of musical rain and then a swell of silvery sound softening to a wail. The swish and swirl of dark and lacy skirts and flicker of slim young limbs, all crimson beauty. There are skies and trickling waters, lifting and falling to music—whispering and crying; soft, so soft, that at last they drift away to utter music almost soundless, pulsing in ecstacy, with now and anon the rough whir and roll of the recovering bass, out of which the silvery music emerges—re-born, alive, wailing, dancing and dying—

I slept the night fitfully with quivering nerves and rose hurriedly—for I had a deed. You see I was tired from talking into the burning eyes of 3,000 school children on yesterday, and from the holy revel of the night, and I had to get to Huntington. There are three lines—two round-about and slow; one, the Chesapeake & Ohio, direct, but through "Jim Crow" Kentucky. I hurried to the city ticket office. Useless—the clerk lied suavely—"the diagram is at the depot—you can easily get a seat there." I did not try. I knew. I walked straight to the Pullman with a porter. The conductor was rough and curt. "Go to the ticket office—I can't sell you a seat." I

From *The Crisis* 23 (April 1922): 249–250. [The two men mentioned in this story are Wendell Phillips Dabney of Cincinnati, a newspaperman and author, and Charles S. Gilpin, a renowned actor. See the index to H. Aptheker, *Annotated Bibliography of the Published Writings of W.E.B. Du Bois* (Millwood, N.Y.: Kraus-Thomson Organization Limited, 1973) for further references to both men.—ED.]

hesitated. There we stood: a depot porter with golden face and sombre eyes; a black inscrutable train porter. A big fat angry white conductor. Then I girded myself for War. "You can assign me when the diagram comes," I said. "Put the bags on." I stumbled on through the car aflame and bitter. I sank to an empty corner seat. Suppose he continued to refuse. The car was filling. I would buy the whole drawing-room—it was taken, just then. We moved across the slimy Ohio to Kentucky. Ah! he would have me there—Law and Gospel against me. But I stuck, grim, with throbbing temples. After a thousand years, he slouched in: "Pullman ticket!" he growled.

"I have none—a seat to Huntington."

"$1.20," he mumbled.

It was over and I had won. I leaned back. The thoughtful porter brought me a pillow. I closed my eyes and listened again to the dim seductive strains of the Spanish Fandango.

57

The Great Surgeon

The tall and beautiful hospital rose white and pure beside the taller and more beautiful cathedral; so that the silvery bell voices of matins and vespers out of cloud-swathed spires woke the sick and the dead daily to want Life and Joy, behind the purple Curtains of Pain. Within, the white and starched and immaculate Superintendent of Nurses towered slim and handsome amid the murmurous applause of a hundred white and starched and immaculate nurses. (Below in the half-cellar, where the steam hissed and curled, a score of black women on tired feet, with sweating tubercular bosoms and great, gnarled hands worked all day each day to keep these brilliant, beautiful things above, immaculate.)

"It is a shame!" said the Superintendent of Nurses. "It is a shame!" echoed half a hundred voices. "The idea of a Jew operating at St. Michael's!"

"It's a shame!' swore the Head Surgeon in his Holy of Holies, beyond the Nurses' hall. "No Jew has ever operated in this hospital."

'And I thought," whispered the Junior Surgeon, kowtowing, "that our Patron was equally strict and steadfast for 'Anglo Saxon supremacy'."

"He was—he was. 'No Jews, Japs, or Negroes', he has said to me again and again—never on the Staff and as seldom in the wards as possible."

"And what has changed him?" asked the Superintendent of Nurses as she glided in, shining and cooing with the faint rustle that suggested wings.

"He's sick. He's sick unto death. He wants to be healed. He's scared blue—and he meets this quack."

" 'The Great Surgeon' the advertisements call him, and they say that the deaf hear, the blind see, and the crippled walk!"

"Yes, and Fools and their money part."

"His charges are ridiculously low."

"Precisely—he is unprofessional; he advertises—whole pages in the *Journal* and *News* with 'Come unto me, all ye that labor,' and such tommy-rot. He rents no offices and has no dignity; he roams the streets of the yellow East Side and the red West Side and black High Harlem. You can see him any day talking with harlots, touts and cripples, thieves, merchants and peddlers, grinning children, dogs and stray cats."

"But," said the House Surgeon, "if your Millionaire wants him—why—"

"He'll have him of course. But think of the reputation of St. Michael's!"

"What ails the old man anyway?"

"Damned if I know."

"The quack says it's Stone."

From *The Crisis* 25 (December 1922): 58–60.

"Then Stone let it be. The man who gives us a hundred thousand a year can have Stone in the Head if he wants it,—and his will is properly made."

"He comes—" "He comes! He is here!"

"What—already? It's ony 1:50. Whoever heard of a surgeon ahead of time! It's not professional."

He came gowned in soft black, afoot, across the snow, up the stairs into the hall. He was short and square, bald with a fringe of black curly hair. His face was sallow, heavy and lined, and his blue eyes burned. (But his hands his great and sinewy hands, calloused, thick, powerful, yet light, quick, with flattened finger tips and ever moving. The nurses rubbed their palms together, mimicking him behind his broad back.)

Beside him moved a shadow—a small, thin, scrawny, almost shabby, man with tender eyes and a great reticule of papers, packages, pads, and pencils. He said no word. He looked.

Below in the private parlor, ministered to by the Superintendent of Nurses and two attendant sprites, sat the rich and furred wife and daughter, waiting. They wore a quarter pound of gold, three ounces of platinum, 13 diamonds, 6 pearls, one sapphire and one ruby, 25 yards of silk, two gorgeous plumes from mangled mothers of starving birds, twenty little fur coats of murdered martens and thirty pieces of silver fox.

"I tried to dissuade him—I cannot understand. It is some spell that this Jew has cast over him. We met him last Saturday, in the street where we were motoring as a short cut—a horrible street, dark, dirty and teeming. This Jew peered in at our window and my husband, groaning in sudden pain, muttered:

" 'What shall I do to be saved!'

"And the Jew said, 'Follow me' and despite all I could do, my husband went."

"Ah—well, but it may be all right—and the Head Surgeon will stand by," murmured the beautiful Superintendent.

"If it isn't all right—if it isn't all right—"

(The time passed by in mighty, sonorous pageant. An hour, in slow and stately tread, while the red sun of heaven burned the azure to darker, blanker blue. A half hour, in slower lagging pace, muffled in tread, thunderous in silence. And then fifteen myriad minutes of quivering hesitation with the twisting, flying, retreating, trailing, pounding of foot-sore pilgrims oozing blood. Then Time stopped and Visions came—knives slipping, cutting, maiming; blood pouring—Horror and Pain and Death—)

The Head Surgeon came down the stairs muttering:

"He would not let me stay in the room. He put the nurses out. He used no ether. It is—horrible. It is murder. Yet listening, I heard no cry nor groan."

"Good God!" gasped the Superintendent.

"Good God," answered the Great Surgeon as he entered noiseless, his vestments ghostly in dull grey white, his lips smiling, his eyes inscrutable.

Wheeling the women faced him. They strove for speech and he made no move to help.

"He will—live?" The wife faltered, at last.

And the Great Surgeon whispered:

"He will die!"

Then the woman rose and shrieked:

"Murderer! Quack! Accused Jew! King of the Jews! Lynch him! Crucify him!"

And she sank mumbling and sobbing into her daughter's arms. But the daughter, pale and straight, said:

"Shut up, Mother!" And then to him, a voice wreathed in hate: "Lead us to him."

Softly through hushed corridors, he led them, stepping lightly, almost joyously, with half-closed eyes and moving lips. Vespers rang sweetly above the falling snow without. Within angel-like forms, white-winged and lovely, flitted dimly, silently. (Below in the cellar the steam hissed and the irons flew and the black women coughed and sighed.)

At the top of the staircase, he did not turn right to the beautiful and expensive private rooms, but left to the general ward of the poor. The wife tottered, beating her hands in frantic disgust. The daughter gasped:

"In the public ward?"

"In the general ward!" fumed the Superintendent.

"He wished it," said the Great Surgeon

And there they found him; there in the dying sunlight with fifty others, sick, maimed and crippled lying about him (and one stiff corpse screened in, afar) lay the mighty Patron, the richest man of all the rich city, dying. The shadowy clerk was perched beside him, sealing a long parchment with a blood-red seal.

The face of the dying man was alight, blazing with the pale glory of the dying sun. There were lilies beside him. Wide bowls of rare and costly lilies, spreading weird fragrance, reflecting the sun and falling snow.

Wearily, yet peacefully, he raised his dying hands—"Mother—old woman," he murmured fondly as he found her: "Daughter—honey! You are poor. You have left but the things on your backs. I have sold all my goods and restored them to the Poor. I have taken this hospital from the Rich and given it to the Son of Man—to the sons of men: to the good and the bad, the black and the white, Jew and Gentile—all human kind of every race and creed."

("He is crazy—crazy!" sobbed the wife. "We'll break the will," hissed the daughter. "The testament, perhaps, but not his Holy Will," said the Surgeon.)

The dying voice fell and whispered:

"All and for all."

The Patron paused and gasped:

"Especially for—Jews—and 'Niggers'." And he died.

The Great Surgeon closed the old and weary eyes of the dead potentate and folded the fat, big hands upon his wounded heart and lighted soft candles at his head and feet. And then slowly he passed down the ward whispering, intoning, to either side as he went: "Peace—Peace be with you." And there followed him his shadow and a murmur and a sigh like far off seas at sunset.

Down in the hall below they stood as if paralysed, while the Great Surgeon, shadowed by his clerk, moved toward the snow-drifts and the starlit night. The Head Surgeon dropped his eyes. The Superintendent of Nurses stared, fascinated. The nurses flew, fluttered and were still.

Only an interne—the Last Interne, hastened noiselessly and threw back the great and oaken door.

"He is—dead, Sir?" he asked.

The Surgeon said: "He that believeth in Me, though he were dead, yet shall he live; and whosoever liveth and believeth in Me shall never die!"

"Then—what ailed him, Sir?"

The Great Surgeon answered softly: "Stone. Stone in the Heart!"

(Below in the half cellar twenty black women twined their dark cloaks about them, swathed their tired feet in riven rubbers, clasped gnarled hands on aching chests, and went up singing to the night.)

So the Eve of Christmas fell on the world in the year of salvation 1922: First came the Master, haloed in the gleaming snow; then his Shadow. And then the pain-swept Song of Angels.

58

On Being Crazy

It was one o'clock and I was hungry. I walked into a restaurant, seated myself and reached for the bill-of-fare. My table companion rose.

"Sir," said he, "do you wish to force your company on those who do not want you?"

No, said I, I wish to eat.

"Are you aware, Sir, that this is social equality?"

Nothing of the sort, Sir, it is hunger,—and I ate.

The day's work done, I sought the theatre. As I sank into my seat, the lady shrank and squirmed.

I beg pardon, I said.

"Do you enjoy being where you are not wanted?" she asked coldly.

Oh no I said.

"Well you are not wanted here."

I was surprised. I fear you are mistaken, I said. I certainly want the music and I like to think the music wants me to listen to it.

"Usher," said the lady, "this is social equality."

No, madame, said the usher, it is the second movement of Beethoven's Fifth Symphony.

After the theatre, I sought the hotel where I had sent my baggage. The clerk scowled.

"What do you want?" he asked.

Rest, I said.

"This is a white hotel," he said.

I looked around. Such a color scheme requires a great deal of cleaning, I said, but I don't know that I object.

"We object," said he.

Then why—, I began, but he interrupted.

"We don't keep 'niggers'," he said, "we don't want social equality."

Neither do I. I replied gently, I want a bed.

I walked thoughtfully to the train. I'll take a sleeper through Texas. I'm a bit dissatisfied with this town.

"Can't sell you one."

I only want to hire it, said I, for a couple of nights.

"Can't sell you a sleeper in Texas," he maintained. "They consider that social equality."

I consider it barbarism, I said, and I think I'll walk.

From *The Crisis* 26 (June 1923): 56–57.

Walking, I met a wayfarer who immediately walked to the other side of the road where it was muddy. I asked his reasons.

" 'Niggers' is dirty," he said.

So is mud, said I. Moreover I added, I am not as dirty as you—at least, not yet.

"But you're a 'nigger', ain't you?" he asked.

My grandfather was so-called.

"Well then!" he answered triumphantly.

Do you live in the South? I persisted, pleasantly.

"Sure," he growled, "and starve there."

I should think you and the Negroes might get together and vote out starvation.

"We don't let them vote."

We? Why not? I said in surprise.

" 'Niggers' is too ignorant to vote."

But, I said, I am not so ignorant as you.

"But you're a 'nigger'."

Yes, I'm certainly what you mean by that.

"Well then!" he returned, with that curiously inconsequential note of triumph. "Moreover," he said, "I don't want my sister to marry a nigger."

I had not seen his sister, so I merely murmured, let her say, no.

"By God you shan't marry her, even if she said yes."

But,—but I don't want to marry her, I answered a little perturbed at the personal turn.

"Why not!" he yelled, angrier than ever.

Because I'm already married and I rather like my wife.

"Is she a 'nigger'?" he asked suspiciously.

Well, I said again, her grandmother—was called that.

"Well then!" he shouted in that oddly illogical way.

I gave up. Go on, I said, either you are crazy or I am.

"We both are," he said as he trotted along in the mud.

59

The Gospel According to St. John, Chapter 12

"*And Martha served.*"

The President of the State Federation of Colored Women's Clubs was in town. She had spoken Christmas afternoon for the local club in the First Baptist Church; and she had spoken sharply and dispassionately. The State Juvenile House of Detention for Colored Girls and Boys was not receiving proper support from the women. Of course the State ought to support it wholly; but the point was the State did not; and the women had promised. They had not kept their promise. Monies had been wasted and frittered away; proper reports had not been made. She appealed to these women in the name of motherhood and in the name of the Christ Child—help! Help till it hurt! She stood there quivering with the fervency of her appeal. And Mary sat at her feet, rapt, transfigured, quivering in response. She saw a woman, tall, fat and brown, heavyfaced with thin, grey hair, with tired lines beneath her eyes, with a countenance that flamed and glowed in her enthusiasm and then settled back into drab disillusion and disappointment. Especially Mary looked at her hands, the hard, sinewy hands of a working woman—one encased in silk, the other, working and gripping with its plain gold ring.

"*And Martha served.*"

She had fried chicken beautifully browned, mashed potatoes and hot biscuit, light and flaky; and sweet potatoes, corn pudding, Smithfield ham and a great, fat juicy mince pie, sizzling; and coffee and cider; and one of the new fruit salads which she had read about in the *Delineator*. The kitchen blazed and the sweat streamed from her little, thin, sharp face as she rushed here and there, for already the guests were gathering. And where was Mary? Mary who should help; Mary the scattered-brained, who was always late; Mary the lovable, thriftless dreamer. Martha hurried in, damp and breathless, to greet Madam President when she arrived, and the Baptist and Methodist ministers, Madam Secretary, Madam Treasurer and a half dozen others—and then hurried back to the kitchen. Where could Mary be?

"*And Martha served.*"

She piled the great golden dish of chicken before Madam President and the Smithfield ham before the Baptist minister and lined the vegetables in brave array between. Where could Mary be? She ought to be helping this minute with the serving of the dinner.

"Now come on out," said Martha. "And all be seated and help yourselves."

The grace was scarcely said when Mary came.

From *The Crisis* 27 (December 1923): 55–56.

"And Martha served."

She brought in the little dishes, the gravy, the butter, the sauce for the salad. Mary rushed in impetuously and stood a moment, starry-eyed, framed in the double doorway between the parlor and the dining room, with a bundle in her arms. Then, with laughter that was almost hysterical, she ran and kneeled at the feet of Madam President.

"You were wonderful, wonderful!" she said as she held her bundle up and thrust it forward. The enveloping papers fell, waving away like stiff, thin clouds before the sun, and up rose the flowers. It was a mass of flowers such as kings look upon and smile—a great glorious burst of color and odor. Cream-swept roses were there in bud and blossom; great crimson poinsettias, pale purple orchids, fine white lilies in bells, and all about the green and threads of fern.

"And the house was filled with the odor."

The guests stared. Madam Secretary choked with indignation; Madam Treasurer laid her biscuit carefully back on her plate.

"It's a shame," she whispered to the Baptist minister, "to waste money like that." The minister smiled and answered:

"Why was not this ointment sold for three hundred pence and given to the poor?"

Madam Treasurer stared at him.

"Three hundred cents? Nonsense," she hissed. "It cost twenty-five dollars, if it cost a cent."

But Madam President had pushed her food aside and placed the flowers in a pitcher before her and her face was transfigured.

"I always loved flowers," she stammered. "I love them so."

"And Martha served."

"And where on earth have you been, Mary?" she rasped. But Madam President said:

"Let her alone. Against the day of my burying hath she kept this. For the poor always ye have with you but me, ye have not always."

And two great tears swelled in her eyes.

60

Little Portraits of Africa

THE PLACE, THE PEOPLE

Africa is vegetation. It is the riotous, unbridled bursting life of leaf and limb. It is sunshine—pitiless shrine of blue rising from morning mists and sinking to hot night shadows. And then the stars—very near are the stars to Africa, near and bright and curiously arrayed. The tree is Africa. The strong, blinding strength of it—the wide deep shade, the burly lavish height of it. Animal life is there wild and abundant—perhaps in the inner jungle I should note it more but here the herb is triumphant, savagely sure—such beautiful shrubbery, such splendor of leaf and gorgeousness of flower I have never seen.

And the people! Last night I went to Kru-town and saw a Christmas masque. There were young women and men of the color of warm ripe horse chestnuts, clothed in white robes and turbaned. They played the Christ story with sincerity, naiveté and verve. Conceive "Silent Night" sung in Kru by this dark white procession with flaming candles; the little black mother of Christ crossing with her baby, in figured blue, with Joseph in Mandingan fez and multi-colored cloak and beside them on her worshipping knees the white wreathed figure of a solemn dark angel. The shepherds watched their flocks by night, the angels sang; and Simeon, raising the baby high in his black arms, sang with my heart in English Kru-wise, *"Lord now lettest thou thy servant depart in peace for mine eyes have seen thy salvation!"*

Liberia is gay in costume—the thrifty Krus who burst into color of a holiday; the proud Veys always well-gowned; the Liberian himself often in white. The children sometimes in their own beautiful skins.

SUNDAY, JANUARY 13, 1924

I have walked three hours in the African bush. In the high bush mighty trees arose draped, with here and there the flash of flower and call of bird. The monkey sentinel cried and his fellows dashed down the great tree avenues. The way was marked—yonder the leopard that called last night under the moon, a bush cow's hoof; a dainty tread of antelope. We leaped the trail of driver ants and poked at the great houses of the white ants. The path rose and wound and fell now soft in green glow, now golden, now shimmery through the water as we balanced on a bare log. There was whine of monkey, scramble of timid unseen life, glide of dark snake. Then came the native farms—coffee, cocoa, plantain, cassava. Nothing is more beautiful

---

From *The Crisis* 27 (April 1924): 273–274.

than an African village—its harmonious colorings—its cleanliness, its dainty houses with the kitchen palaver place of entertainment, its careful delicate decorations and then the people. I believe that the African form in color and curve is the beautifulest thing on earth; the face is not so lovely—though often comely with perfect teeth and shining eyes—but the form of the slim limbs, the muscled torso, the deep full breasts!

The bush is silence. Silence of things to be, silence vocal with infinite minor music and flutter and tremble—but silence, deep silence of the great void of Africa.

And the palms; some rose and flared like green fine work; some flared before they rose; some soared and drooped; some were stars and some were sentinels; then came the ferns—the feathery delicate things of grottos and haunts with us, leapt and sang in the sun—they thrust their virgin tracery up and out and almost to trees. Bizarre shapes of grass and shrub and leaf greeted us as though some artist all Divine was playing and laughing and trying every trick of his bewitched pencil above the mighty buildings of the ants.

I am riding on the singing heads of black boys swinging in a hammock. The smooth black bodies swing and sing, the neck set square, the hips sway. O lovely voices and sweet young souls of Africa!

MONROVIA

Monrovia is a city set upon a hill. With coy African modesty her face is half turned from the bold and boisterous ocean and her wide black eyes gaze dreamfully up the Stockton and St. Paul. Her color is white and green and her head of homes rises slowly and widely in spacious shading verandah toward the great headland of Mesurado where the lighthouse screams to wandering ships. Her hair is plaited decently on mighty palm leaves and mangoes; her bare feet, stained with travel, torn with ancient cicatriced wounds drabble in the harbor waters down on Water Street and shun the mud town Plymouth Rock which is Providence Island. Her feet are ugly and old, but oh her hands, her smooth and black and flying hands are beautiful and they linger on roof and porch, in wide-throated grassy street and always they pat and smooth her hair, the green and sluggish palms of her heavy beautiful hair. And there is gold in her hair.

AFRICA

The spell of Africa is upon me. The ancient witchery of her medicine is burning my drowsy, dreamy blood. This is not a country, it is a world—a universe of itself and for itself, a thing Different, Immense, Menacing, Alluring. It is a great black bosom where the Spirit longs to die. It is life so burning, so fire encircled that one bursts with terrible soul inflaming life. One longs to leap against the sun and then calls, like some great hand of fate, the slow, silent crushing power of almighty sleep—of Silence, of immovable Power beyond, within, around. Then comes the calm. The dreamless beat of midday stillness at dusk, at dawn, at noon, always. Things move—black shiny bodies, perfect bodies, bodies of sleek unearthly poise and beauty. Eyes languish, black eyes—slow eyes, lovely and tender eyes in great dark formless faces. Life is slow here. Impetuous Americans quiver in impetuous graves. I saw where the ocean roars to the soul of Henry Highland Garnet. Life slows down and as it slows it deepens; it rises and descends to immense and secret places. Unknown evil appears and unknown good. Africa is the Spiritual Frontier of human kind—oh the wild and beautiful adventures of its taming! But oh! the cost thereof—the endless, endless cost! Then will come a day—an old and ever, ever young day when there will spring in Africa a civilization without coal, without noise, where machinery will sing and never rush and roar, and where men will sleep and think and dance and lie prone before the rising suns, and women will be happy.

The objects of life will be revolutionized. Our duty will not consist in getting up at seven, working furiously for six, ten and twelve hours, eating in sullen ravenousness or extraordinary repletion. No—We shall dream the day away and in cool dawns, in little swift hours, do all our work.

61

An Interview

I have just had an interview with a young gentleman who desires to remain anonymous. In fact, he was at first rather loth to grant an interview, alleging that he was quite unused to the process. Still, when I spoke of his career he acknowledged that he was "quite a man now. In fact, I will be ten years old next Thursday." After I had solemnly promised, cross-my-heart, not to divulge his identity he consented to talk.

I told him that I understood that he had some success in teaching parents. He said that he had, but that it was a "tough job!" I appealed to him that there were numbers of little kids and babies coming along who needed the benefit of his wisdom. He said that that was probably true.

He impressed it upon me that he thought a great deal of his parents and wouldn't change them for anything.

"You see, they ain't really to blame. They just don't know. They've been away from Heaven so long that they've forgotten all about it. Now I'm sort of new and fresh so I could tell them a few things. But, gee! It was some work to make them understand."

SLEEP

He said that the first lesson that he had to teach his parents was about night and day; and that everybody knows that night is for sleep and day for keeping awake. Well, when he was hardly a week old he found that his folks wanted him apparently to sleep all the time. Of course, he admitted, he was a bit drowsy, what with travelling thousands and thousands and thousands of miles with none too much to eat; but now that he had arrived and was looking around to get acquainted with things, he wanted to see all that he could while there was daylight. Especially he liked the early morning when the sun was getting out of its crib of clouds and little drops of water glistened on the flowers and there was a nice, chilly, cuddly feeling in the world. Always the little birdies called him about that time and he called back as loud as he could and,

"What do you think?" he said, "Dad would growl and snort and thrash about and Mumsy would cry, 'Hush, hush,' and try to smother me and sing me to sleep at five o'clock in the morning! Could you beat it?"

He just got mad and yelled and kept up the yelling. He told his parents in as plain English as he could master, that it was time to be up and asked them what they supposed God made day for anyway. This first lesson of his parents took some time, but after a few months they consented to serve breakfast at five and to let him lie and

From *The Crisis* 28 (October 1924): 248–250.

sing to himself. Of course, he was really singing to the angels and they were singing back and he wanted to have his parents hear and talk to them about it but they were always drunk with sleep.

MEALS

The next big lesson that he remembered was about meals. His parents seemed to have the idea that eating was not very important except when they happened to think of it. Of course he knew better. He knew that the first duty of babies is to eat and eat often and eat on time; so that when meals were late he proceeded to raise Ned and it didn't make any difference to him whether visitors were present or Mother was busy or Mrs. Jones was on the phone. It was eating time and he had to eat. He said he knew it was selfish but that you had just got to be selfish if you were ever going to grow up.

"My stomach hurts something awful when it's empty and I am liable to get sick and weak and dead if I don't eat on time."

It took him about a year to teach this lesson to his parents.

BEING LET ALONE

He said that the next lesson was more difficult, perhaps because it was more indefinite. It was about being let alone. He didn't mind one of Mother's soft little kisses now and then or a short hug from Dad if it wasn't too hard; but he did seriously object to being continually pulled and jabbed and squeezed. He didn't like to have strangers sticking their wet mouths all over him. He didn't want to be rolled and tossed and tumbled. He didn't always want to be fixed up and dressed. Sometimes he would almost go wild with too much attention. Just as he was having a pretty dream or a big thought or just as he was trying to remember dimly how the archangel's wings shone by the great white throne, suddenly it would be "Darling this" and "Darling that" and he would be half smothered and so angered that it drove the dream and thought all away. Visitors were especially objectionable on this account. They always wanted to "see the baby"; they always declared he was "cute"; they kept him in most uncomfortable positions while they decided whom he resembled. He said that he learned to crawl, walk and run just to escape these ogres. Sometimes he scratched and bit them. He just had to have some time to himself, if he was to be about his Father's business.

PLAY

He got very much interested when I took up the matter of play. "First eat and then play, that's what a baby's for," he asserted. He declared that parents did not take play seriously unless it was their own play. They forgot about it or they lectured him about it. They didn't mind his toys or didn't buy them. They didn't get the right toys or toys at the right time. They always thought they knew what you wanted to do better than you knew and above all they expected you to play and not get dirty. Now this young gentleman was very dogmatic on the subject of dirt. He affirmed that dirt was natural. "I love mud" was the way he put it. He asserted that the last five years of his life had been given to a struggle to be allowed to be reasonably dirty; that in this terrific battle he had achieved rompers, then gotten rid of lace and curls and finally got the right to play with other children and get as dirty as they did.

"It's funny 'bout other children," he said reflectively. " 'Course I know I'm better than all other children that ever was but why swank about it?" He asserted that there *were* other children and they were the best possible toys to play with and that it was the business of mothers and fathers to furnish such playmates. Brothers and sisters were best because they were always home and ready; but, failing these, children ought to be borrowed and borrowed often and in sufficient quantities. All this took a long time to teach his parents but, said he, "I've got 'em taught. You ought to see the gang in our block!"

FOOLING ME

On the next subject my young gentleman got very solemn. "Why do my parents keep trying to fool me?" he asked. His first indignation on this point came when they gave him rubber things instead of food; when they hid away from him, promising to be "right back"; and especially when they tried to take away the Fairies. That was the worst. He appealed to me as witness that everybody that knows anything knows that there are angels and fairies. Of course he knew it better than most folks because he had so recently come from the place where they live. But it seems that his mother and father were so old that they had forgotten that they had ever seen such things and really thought they were make-believe! So instead of letting the real fairies help them they tried to make up fairies and fairy tales; and our young gentleman had faith in this make-believe until he caught his father playing Santa Claus. Then he really was mad.

A JOKE

And this brought out another phase of his parents' peculiar ignorance which called for all his ingenuity as a teacher. They refused to take him seriously. Just because he was a little man they seemed to think he was a joke. He was always supposed to be funny and to be laughed at. Some great fat stranger would heave into sight and explode into gales of laughter when our young hero appeared. On the other hand if he laughed at the grown ups (and they were awful funny at times), *my!* what a serious thing it was! It took long years and a series of tantrums interspersed by whippings before his parents began to take him seriously.

Just about this time, also, they began to talk English to him. Before that and at the very time when he was trying to learn English, they persisted in talking in extraordinary jargon to him that he couldn't understand and didn't want to understand.

WHIPPINGS

Finally, and with considerable finesse, I mentioned the subject of whippings. The young gentleman did not want to talk on this matter as it seemed to bring up painful memories. Indeed, he told me confidentially, that he had probably received "more'n a million" whippings. I rather doubted that, but I did not dispute him. He acknowledged that some of these whippings were deserved; that he had been bad and knew it and needed a severe reminder. But most of the times, he asserted, he had been whipped primarily because Dad was mad and Mother was tired and he happened to get in the way. A few times he had been whipped when he was not guilty and this had seriously outraged his feelings. He also asserted that "oodles of other times" he had deserved a whipping and had not gotten it because his parents forgot about it or had eaten a good dinner. He asserted that this was all wrong:

"If Dad is going to be God, he must always be right and if he ain't he shouldn't play at it."

He was of opinion that now that he had reached the age of ten, this whipping business would better stop. It was too uncertain and messy. "I don't mind it so much but it's awful hard on Dad and Mumsy."

So that is how I got the distinct idea from this young gentleman that the business of teaching parents is pretty difficult and that we ought not to leave it entirely to the children. As he said, he didn't mind going on with the business. In fact, he'd probably have to; but he had got a lot of things to do for himself in the next ten years and he hated to be bothered with teaching his parents. On the whole, I venture to suggest a school for parents, especially for parents of children from 0 to 10 years of age.

62

The Temptation in the Wilderness

There was a man standing in the Wilderness. He was black and thin and his clothes were shabby but his eyes burned toward heaven.

Then was Jesus led up of the Spirit into the wilderness to be tempted of the devil.

O wide was the wilderness and tangled—dark and full of sounds and silences. He could not understand it—he could not see a way; it baffled him. It was full of work, yet work he could not find. It was full of bread yet he was hungry. It was filled with the Word of God—yet the Word was silence to him. He was twenty years young and the Wilderness stretched from his High Hill of Graduation down yonder to the low gates where one might see the Valley of the Shadow of Death.

And when he had fasted forty days and forty nights, he was afterward ahungered.

And when the tempter came to him he said, If thou be the Son of God, command that these stones be made bread.

Bread? Bread and butter! Yes, he must earn it. The days of the years of his childhood were past. He must turn stones into bread. But not into bread alone. No. Into great cathedrals, into tall temples, into bridges that fly floods. And not stones alone—but Life, Joy, the Spirit and the Word.

The thin black man looked curiously on the tempter. The devil was a woman—young and beautiful; in silk and jewels, with fingers as soft as her voice. He smiled at the devil wanly:

But he answered and said, It is written, Man shall not live by bread alone, but by every word that proceedeth out of the mouth of God.

Ten years with slow and stately tread pass by. The black man is thirty, and his work undone, his life unlived, his hungry soul unsatisfied. The devil is a business man, tailored and groomed:

And the devil, taking him up into a high mountain, showed unto him all the kingdoms of the world in a moment of time.

And the devil said unto him, All this power will I give thee, and the glory of them: for that is delivered unto me; and to whomsoever I will, I give it.

If thou therefore wilt worship me, all shall be thine.

The Kingdoms of the world! The glory of them; like a thread of silver Piccadilly melts into the Strand; like a thread of gold, the Champs Elysées slip to the Bois; Broadway thunders through its canyons; the Prado burns and sings. Above them tower Milan, Woolworth, Taj Mahal, Alhambra and the Opera. North is pine and ice and fur; west is orange and gold; east is oak and silver; south is palm and sea and fire.

From *The Crisis* 29 (December 1924): 58.

All amidst them are jewels and silk, color and curve, music and dance, dream and tale, knowledge and cunning. Ah, the Kingdoms of the World.

And suddenly the glory faded. And suddenly all was dirt and pain and blood; and hate and horror. Which was God and who and what and why? The devil spread his hands. "I am God" he said.

And Jesus answered and said unto him, Get thee behind me, Satan:

Then the devil taketh him up into the holy city, and setteth him on a pinnacle of the temple.

And saith unto him, If thou be the Son of God, cast thyself down; for it is written, He shall give his angels charge concerning thee; and in their hands they shall bear thee up, lest at any time thou dash thy foot against a stone.

The black man was forty and older and thinner. He stared into the Valley of the Shadow of Death. Was he really one of the sons of God? Did his father's angels have charge over him?

Miracles? Were not they the answer? Must not God himself and his angels come and come quickly to earth, to settle this awful problem of color and race? How simple. Stop work. Call God. Come down as avenging prophet, revealing seer, sacrificing saviour. And yet—was it fair to call a busy God,—to tempt him from his own work? Perhaps he too was being crucified! He stared at the devil. The devil was a priest in robe and mitre chanting long prayers.

Jesus said unto him, It is written again, Thou shalt not tempt the Lord thy God.

63

The Black Man Brings His Gifts

We've got a pretty fine town out here in middle Indiana. We claim fifty thousand inhabitants although the census cheats us out of nearly half. You can't depend on those guys in Washington. The new Pennsylvania station has just gone up and looks big and clean although a bit empty on account of the new anti-loafing ordinance. There is a White Way extending down through the business section which makes us quite gay at night. Of course, we have Rotary, Kiwanis, the Chamber of Commerce and the Federation of Women's Clubs. There are six churches, not counting the colored folks.

Well, last year somebody suggested we have an America's Making pageant just like New York. You see, we need something to sort of bring us together after the war. We had a lot of Germans here and near-Germans and we had to pull them up pretty stiff. In all, we had seven or eight races or nations, not counting the colored people. We salute the flag and many of us can sing The Star Spangled Banner without books. But we really need Americanization; a sort of wholesome getting together.

So, as I have said, last year the Federation of Women's Clubs started the matter and got a committee appointed. They appointed me and Birdie; Mrs. Cadwalader Lee (who is an awfully aristocratic Southern lady); Bill Graves, who runs the biggest store; the editor of the daily paper and the Methodist preacher, who has the biggest church. They made me secretary but Birdie suggested that we needed an impartial chairman who knew something about the subject, for, says she, "What with the Germans, Poles, Scandinavians and Italians, everybody will claim so much that there'll be nothing left for the real Americans." We met and considered the idea favorably and wrote to the state university. They sent us down a professor with a funny name and any number of degrees. It seems that he taught sociology and "applied ethics," whatever that may be.

"I'll bet he's a Jew," said Birdie as soon as she looked at him. "I've got nothing against Jews but I just don't like them. They're too pushing."

First thing off the bat, this professor, who wore a cloak and spoke exceedingly proper and too low for anybody to hear unless they were listening, asked if the colored people ought not to be represented. That took us a bit by surprise as we hadn't thought of them at all. Mrs. Cadwalader Lee said she thought it might be best to have a small auxiliary colored committee and that she would ask her cook to get one up.

"Well," says I, after we had gotten nicely settled for our first real meeting, "what is the first thing that's gone to making America and who did it?" I had my own mind

---

From *The Survey* (New York), 53 (March 1, 1925): 655–657, 710.

on music and painting and I know that Birdie is daft on architecture; but before we either of us could speak, Bill Graves grinned and said, "hard work."

The chairman nodded and said, "Quite true, labor."

I didn't know just what to say but I whispered to Birdie that it seemed to me that we ought to stress some of the higher things. The chairman must have heard me because he said that all higher things rested on the foundation of human toil.

"But, whose labor?" asked the editor. "Since we are all descended from working people, isn't labor a sort of common contribution which, as it comes from everybody, need not be counted?"

"I should hardly consent to that statement," said Mrs. Cadwalader Lee, who is said to be descended from a governor and a lord.

"At any rate," said the chairman, "the Negroes were America's first great labor force."

"Negroes!" shrilled Birdie, "but we can't have them!"

"I should think," said Mrs. Cadwalader Lee, softly, "that we might have a very interesting darky scene. Negroes hoeing cotton and that sort of thing." We all were thankful to Mrs. Lee and immediately saw that that would be rather good; Mrs. Lee again said she would consult her cook, a very intelligent and exemplary person.

"Next," I said firmly, "comes music."

"Folk songs," said the Methodist preacher.

"Yes," I continued. "There would be Italian and German and—"

"But I thought this was to be American," said the chairman.

"Sure," I answered, "German-American and Italian-American and so forth."

"There ain't no such animal," says Birdie, but Mrs. Cadwalader Lee reminded us of Foster's work and thought we might have a chorus to sing Old Folks at Home, Old Kentucky Home and Nelly Was a Lady. Here the editor pulled out a book on American folk songs by Krehbiel or some such German name and read an extract. (I had to copy it for the minutes.) It said†:

> The only considerable body of songs which has come into existence in the territory now compassed by the United States, I might even say in North America, excepting the primitive songs of the Indians (which present an entirely different aspect), are the songs of the former black slaves. In Canada the songs of the people, or that portion of the people that can be said still to sing from impulse, are predominantly French, not only in language but in subject. They were for the greater part transferred to this continent with the bodily integrity which they now possess. Only a small portion show an admixture of Indian elements; but the songs of the black slaves of the South are original and native products. They contain idioms which were transplanted from Africa, but as songs they are the product of American institutions; of the social, political and geographical environment within which their creators were placed in America; of the influences to which they were subjected in America; of the joys, sorrows and experiences which fell to their lot in America.
>
> Nowhere save on the plantations of the South could the emotional life which is essential to the development of true folksong be developed; nowhere else was there the necessary meeting of the spiritual cause and the simple agent and vehicle. The white inhabitants of the continent have never been in the state of cultural ingenuousness which prompts spontaneous emotional utterances in music.

This rather took our breath and the chairman suggested that the auxiliary colored committee might attend to this. Mrs. Cadwalader Lee was very nice about it.

(She has such lovely manners and gets her dresses direct from New York.) She said that she was sure it could all be worked out satisfactorily. We would need a number of servants and helpers. Well, under the leadership of that gifted cook, we'd have a cotton-hoeing scene to represent labor and while hoeing they would sing Negro ditties; afterward they could serve the food and clean up.

That was fine, but I didn't propose to be sidetracked.

"But," I says, "we don't want to confine ourselves to folk songs. There is a lot of splendid American music like that of Victor Herbert and Irving Berlin."

The editor grinned. But the chairman was real nice and he mentioned several folks I never heard of—Paine, Buck, Chadwick and DeKoven. And, of course, I know of Nevin and McDowell. Still that editor grinned and said, "Yes, and Harry Burleigh and W. C. Handy and Nathaniel Dett."

Here the preacher spoke up. "I especially like that man, Dett. Our choir sang his Listen to the Lambs last Christmas."

"Oh, yes," said Mrs. Cadwalader Lee, "and Burleigh's Young Warrior was one of the greatest of our war songs."

"I am sure," said the Methodist preacher, "that our choir will be glad to furnish the music."

"But are they colored?" asked the chairman, who had been silent.

"Colored?" we gasped.

"Well, you see, each race was to furnish its own contribution."

"Yes," we chorused, "but this is white American music."

"Not on your life," said the editor, who is awfully slangy. "Of course you know Burleigh and Dett and Handy are all Negroes."

"I think you're mistaken," said Mrs. Cadwalader Lee, getting a bit red in the face.

But sure enough, the chairman said they were and we did not dare dispute him. He even said that Foster's melodies were based on Negro musical themes.

"Well," said the preacher, "I am sure there are no Negroes in town who could sing Listen to the Lambs," and the editor added, "And I hardly think your choir could render The Memphis Blues just as it ought to be." We looked at each other dubiously and I saw right then and there that America's Making had a small chance of being put on in our town. Somebody said that there was a choir in one of the colored churches that could sing this music, but Mrs. Cadwalader Lee reminded us that there would be insuperable difficulties if we tried to bring in obstreperous and high-brow Negroes who demanded social equality. It seems that one of these churches had hired a new social worker—a most objectionable colored person who complained when Mrs. Lee called her by her first name.

"That editor is just lugging the Negroes in," said I to Birdie.

"The Negroes seem to be lugging us in," she replied, and she launched us into architecture. From architecture we went to painting. There were Sargent and Whistler and Abbey. Birdie had seen Tanner's Raising of Lazarus in the Luxembourg and suggested a tableau.

"We might get him to help," said the editor. "He's having an exhibit in New York." We were thrilled, all except Mrs. Lee. "I understand he has Negro blood," she said coldly, "and besides, I do not think much of his work." We dropped that and hurried to inventions.

Here, of course, America is preeminent and we must pick and choose. First the preacher asked what kinds of inventions we ought to stress since America was so very inventive. Bill Graves wanted to stress those which had made big money, while the preacher wanted to emphasize those which had "made for righteousness." Birdie said she was strong for those which were really helpful and the chairman suggested the telephone, things that had helped travel, labor-saving devices, etc.

Well, we named over a number of things and especially stressed the telephone. The editor mentioned Granville Wood as one who had helped to perfect the telephone but we didn't listen. I'm sure he was a Negro. But in spite of all, the chairman spoke up again.

"Shoes," he said.

"Well," said I, "I didn't know we invented shoes. I thought they were pretty common before America was discovered."

"But American shoes are the best in the world," said the editor, and then the chairman told us of the United Shoe Machinery Company and how they made shoes.

"And," he added, "that lasting machine which is at the bottom of their success was invented by a Negro."

"I don't believe it," said Birdie flatly, looking at Mrs. Cadwalader Lee. Mrs. Lee got pale this time.

"Of course," she said, "if you are just going to drag in the Negro by the ears—"

"Still," said the editor, "we are after the truth, ain't we? And it is certainly true that Matzeliger invented the lasting machine and you wouldn't want your sister to marry Matzeliger, now would you?"

"Ain't he dead?" asked Birdie, and Mrs. Cadwalader Lee doubted if we ought to be interested in anything as common as shoes.

"I should think automobiles and locomotives would express our genius better."

"Only, we didn't invent them," said the editor.

"But we did invent a method of oiling them while in motion," said the chairman.

"And I'll bet a colored man did that," said Birdie.

"Quite true," answered the chairman. "His name was Elijah McCoy. He is still living in Detroit and I talked with him the other day."

"Might I ask," said Mrs. Cadwalader Lee, looking the chairman full in the face, "if you yourself are of pure white blood?" We all started and we looked the chairman over. He was of dark complexion and his hair was none too straight. He had big black eyes that did not smile much; and yet there couldn't be any doubt about his being white. Wasn't he a professor in the state university and would they hire a colored men no matter how much he knew? The chairman answered.

"I do not know about the purity of my blood although I have usually been called white. Still, one never knows," and he looked solemnly at Mrs. Cadwalader Lee.

Of course, I rushed in, angels being afraid, and cried,

"Dancing—we haven't provided for dancing and we ought to have a lot of that."

"Lovely," says Birdie, "I know a Mexican girl who can do a tango and we could have folk-dancing for the Irish and Scotch."

"The Negroes invented the tango as well as the cake walk and the whole modern dance craze is theirs," said the editor.

This time the preacher saved us. "I'm afraid," said he, "that I could not countenance public dancing. I am aware that our church has changed its traditional attitude somewhat, but I am old-fashioned. If you are to have dancing—" We hastened to reassure him unanimously. We would have no dancing. We dropped it then and there.

Mrs. Lee now spoke up. "It seems to me," she said, "that the real greatness of America lies in her literature. Not only the great writers like Poe and Lanier but in our folk-lore. There are the lovely legends of the mountain whites and, of course, the Uncle Remus tales. I sometimes used to recite them and would not be unwilling to give my services to this pageant."

"Negro dialect, aren't they?" asked the editor, with vast innocence.

"Yes," said Mrs. Lee, "but I am quite familiar with the dialect."

"But oughtn't they to be given by a Negro?" persisted the editor.

"Certainly not; they were written by a white man, Joel Chandler Harris."

"Yes," added the chairman, "he set them down, but the Negroes originated them—they are thoroughly African."

Mrs. Cadwalader Lee actually sniffed. "I am sorry," she said, "but it seems to me that this matter has taken a turn quite different from our original purpose and I'm afraid I may not be able to take part." This would kill the thing, to my mind, but Birdie was not sure.

"Oh, I don't know," she whispered, "she is too high-brow anyway and this thing ought to be a matter of the common people. I don't mind having a few colored people take part so long as they don't want to sit and eat with us; but I do draw the line on Jews."

Well, we took up education next and before we got through, in popped Booker T. Washington. And then came democracy and it looked like everybody had had a hand in that, even the Germans and Italians. The chairman also said that two hundred thousand Negroes had fought for their own liberty in the Civil War and in the war to make the world safe for democracy. But that didn't impress Mrs. Lee or any of the rest of us and we concluded to leave the Negro out of democracy.

"First thing you know you'll have us eating with Negroes," said Birdie, and the chairman said that he'd eaten with Republicans and sinners. I suppose he meant to slur Democrats and Socialists but it was a funny way to do it. Somehow I couldn't just figure out that chairman. I kept watching him.

Then up pops that editor with a lot of notes and papers. "What about exploration?" he asks. Well, we had forgotten that, but naturally the Italians could stage a good stunt with Columbus.

"And the French and Spanish," said Birdie, "only there are none of them in town, thank God!"

"But there are colored folk!" said that chairman. I just gave him a withering look.

"Were they Columbus' cooks?" I asked.

"Probably," said the chairman, "but the one I have in mind discovered New Mexico and Arizona. But I'm afraid," he added slowly, "that we're getting nowhere."

"We've already got there," said Birdie. But the chairman continued: "How could we when we're talking for people and not letting them express themselves?"

"But aren't we the committee?" I asked.

"Yes, and by our own appointment."

"But we represent all the races," I insisted, "except, well—except the Negroes."

"Just so," replied the chairman, "and while I may seem to you to be unduly stressing the work of Negroes, that is simply because they are not represented here. I promise to say nothing further on the matter if you will indulge me a few minutes. In the next room, a colored woman is waiting. She is that social worker at the colored church and she is here by my invitation, I had hoped to have her invited to sit on this committee. As that does not seem possible, may she say just a word?"

He looked at me. I looked at Birdie and Birdie stared at Mrs. Cadwalader Lee. Mrs. Lee arose.

"Certainly—oh, certainly," she said sweetly. "Don't let me interfere. But, of course, you will understand that we Lees must draw the line somewhere," and out she sailed.

I knew the whole thing was dead as a door nail and I was just about to tell Birdie so when in marched that Negro before we'd had a chance to talk about her. She had on a tailor-made gown that cost fifty dollars if a cent, a smart toque and (would you believe it?) she was a graduate of the University of Chicago! If there's anything I hate it's a college woman. And here was a black one at that. I didn't know just how to treat her so I sort of half turned my shoulder to her and looked out the window. She began with an essay. It had a lot of long words which sounded right even if they weren't. What she seemed to be driving at was this:

Who made this big country? Not the millionaires, the ministers and the "know-alls," but laborers and drudges and slaves. And she said that we had no business to forget this and pretend that we were all descended from the nobility and gentry and college graduates. She even went so far as to say that cranks and prostitutes and plain fools had a hand in making this republic, and that the real glory of America was what it proved as to the possibilities of common-place people and that the hope of the future lay right in these every-day people.

It was the truth and I knew it and so did all of us, but, of course, we didn't dare to let on to each other, much less to her. So I just kept staring out the window and she laid aside her essay and began to talk. She handed to the Negro, music, painting sculpture, drama, dancing, poetry and letters. She named a lot of people I never heard of; and others like Dunbar and Braithwaite and Chesnutt, but I had always thought they were white. She reminded us of Bert Williams and told us of some fellows named Aldridge and Gilpin.

And then she got on our nerves. She said all this writing and doing beautiful things hurt. That it was born of suffering. That sometimes the pain blurred the message, but that the blood and crying lurked beneath. And at last she took out a little thin black book and read.

She read about this country not belonging to white folks any more than it did to black folks and that the black folks got here before the pilgrims. I couldn't help stepping on Birdie's toes because she says her people came in on some boat named after a flower so long ago she's forgot their names. The black girl said that the story of the Negro could be found on every page of the story of America. This made me sick and I turned and glared right at her. But she looked right through me and went on. She said Negroes had been soldiers in all our wars, had nursed the babies, cooked the food and sung and danced besides working so hard that "working like a nigger" was about the hardest work you could picture.

And she asked us if America could have been America without Negroes.

She had me up a tree, I must admit. And I reckon the rest felt as I did—all except that editor.

The chairman looked at us with owl-like eyes; then he shoved a paper at me and read it aloud as he did:

"Timeo Nigros et dona ferentes."‡

Nobody knows what he meant and nobody gave him the satisfaction of asking.

Well, we just sat and stared until she left. Then we went on talking but we didn't touch the real question; and that was, could we have America's Making without Mrs. Cadwalader Lee and with the Negroes?

We couldn't make up our minds and before we had courage to say so openly we went smash on religion.

We might possibly have had some sort of an America's Making pageant if we hadn't discussed religion. You see, the editor who is downright malicious and hates the Federation of Women's Clubs because they start things, got us all wrong by trying to get a definition of religion. He was strong on meekness and humility and turning the other cheek and that sort of thing and I know he didn't mean a word of it.

"I suppose," said Birdie, "that you'll be saying that the Negroes have given us all our religion because they're cowards and allowed themselves to be slaves and take insult today meekly."

"I must admit," said the preacher, "that if the meek inherit the earth, the American Negro will get a large share."

"But will the meek inherit the earth?" I asked.

"I think so," said the chairman calmly.

Birdie jumped up and reached for her cloak. "I believe you're a Jew and a pacifist," she said.

"I am both," he answered.

"And I suppose," said I, getting my hat on straight, "that when somebody slaps you over, you turn the other cheek."

"I did," said he.

"Well, you're a fool," I answered, reaching for my coat.

And Birdie yelled, "And what did they do to you after you turned the other cheek? Answer me that?"

"They crucified me," said the chairman.

EDITOR'S NOTES
†Du Bois is quoting H. E. Krehbiel, *Afro-American Folk-Songs* (New York: Schirmer, 1913).

‡"I fear the Negroes and throw them to the beasts."

64

Georgia

Mine eyes have seen the Pageant of the Progress of Georgia, from Atlanta to the sea. First come the millionaires—strong, quick and tailored men. Their faces are white-washed walls. Their brains are counting machines clicking unchanging and immutable Truth. Their hearts are chips from that Stone Mountain where Daughters of the Confederacy are making the memory of the War for Slavery eternal.

After the millionaires hurry the Harlots—skeletons in rags of silk with gold and jewels rattling on their bones. Whether their faces were black or white one may not know; but on their gaping skulls lie powder, paint and tears.

After the Harlots come the Children—children of the mills, children of the fields, all the thousands and thousands of children whom there are no school-rooms to hold. There is no laughter in these children's eyes. They trudge along. The white ones despise the black. The black ones hate the white. Both starve in body and soul.

After the Children—the Church. First the church that is White, with grave and silent men, with pious and silent women; with Bible and gospel hymn book and Fundamental Creed. They ignore the church that is Black with mighty ignorance. They carry a long noosed rope and the rope lashing backward caresses a Cross. Beneath the Cross staggers an old and weary Jew whom once the World lynched. He was called the Christ.

Behind the Christ dances the church that is Black. It smiles at the church that is White. It helps Christ carry his Cross.

Behind the Church float shadows. Within the shadows soft voices sing a great Music wherein the murmur of all the rivers of Georgia blends in sombre sympathy with the Sorrow Song of slaves. Above the shadows I see the rising sun.

From *The Crisis* 30 (August 1925): 165.

65

The Son of God

Joe struck her hard, right in the face. Mary swayed back a little toward the bureau, but said nothing and stood slim and straight. He wanted to hit her again and started to, but he could not. It was extraordinary how she always impressed him. Those black somber pupils set in the ivory white of her eyes; the rich smooth brown skin and above, the nimbus of grey-black hair, lifted like an aureole. She gave an extraordinary impression of innocence, purity and power, in spite of all he knew,—in spite of what she had just told him.

"Why the hell don't you tell me who his father is?" he snarled again, feeling all the while his first revulsion and anger ebbing slowly away. But Mary only repeated slowly what she had said before:

"He is the Son of God!"

So Joe turned and stormed out into the night. He couldn't make it out. What would the fellows say? How had he come to marry this black girl anyway? He hadn't meant to; but somehow she fascinated him; the curving beauty of her perfect form; the delicate softness of her skin; the dark and secret brooding that ever lurked in her eyes. Besides, he had wanted to get married. He wanted to be decent and have a family, and now here was this mess. Here she was already with child and she had told him so after he had married her. Well, he'd get rid of her and damned quick. He would drive her out. Then he thought of the new cottage with a sharp twinge of regret. Of course it wasn't so much,—only two rooms; but it was new; it was his. He had built it himself with her sitting by, singing low songs. It was in a sense the masterpiece of an untutored but earnest artist.

And now this had to come. He couldn't figure it out. He couldn't see what had gotten into her. She never went with anybody but him. It had been hard at first even to get her to look at him. He clenched his hands, striding through the fields, across the branch and up the hill into the sun-set. If it was some of that damned white trash beyond the hill he would have to kill him, of course; but somehow he knew it wasn't. But who else could it be? None of the colored boys had dared look at her since he had marked her for his own.

Then somehow as the weeks passed the pain and bitterness of it faded away. He couldn't make up his mind what he ought to do. There was that air of still and pure loveliness about her; inexplicable, contradictory, unworldly. Uncanny it was, but there. And so he did nothing but waited in surly pain; and late in December, the boy was born, and Joe was holding him wonderingly in his arms, while she lay strait and terrible still. At first, he groaned for he thought her dead but she opened her calm,

From *The Crisis* 40 (December 1933): 276–277.

dark eyes and fixed them on him. And her eyes spoke,—and he knew that she was saying again:

"He is the Son of God."

As weeks and months passed, that happened which he was sure never could happen. The child became his child; he loved it passionately, and it was only when he was angry or a little drunk that he could remember that it wasn't his. Then he swore at Mary or sulked or demanded angrily again: "Who's his father anyway?" It was marvelous, the fascination of that wee bit of life; the soft perfection of its body; the light that grew daily in its eyes; the little curling tendrils of its hair. There came the days of its first teeth and its standing alone. Its little low gurgles of delight, its wild griefs, and the outstretching of its arms.

Naturally Joe wanted, and yet he did not want the boy named after him; it ought to be and of a surety it ought not to be. "No," he said one day. "Call it what you damned please. But not Joe—not after me." So she called it Joshua and for months Joe searched his memory and the country round for a Joshua; but he found none.

And always silently to and fro went the slim mother, like a certain dark and silver wisp of summer rain or a shadow upon a sun-lit hill. She talked little and yet she listened and put the answering word in just where it made Joe know that she was listening and understanding. Of his work, of his trouble, the old plow, the lame mule, the vagaries of the second-hand Ford, and the boy. Then slowly, she smiled. It always ended there as so often he did not mean it should. It always ended with the boy. For still and always to her, he was the Son of God.

Joshua grew into a silent, brooding but infinitely sympathetic child, whose smile was benediction. He asked few questions and took no orders, and went his own still way. Joe always remembered with a grim satisfaction about the boy at Quarterly meeting. Joshua was twelve then and had already incurred the bitter dislike of the Methodist preacher, whom he had very calmly but decisively disputed in Sunday School. Joe was tickled. He hated that preacher anyway. Always interfering. Sure, he might be right. Probably was. But he had no business to be so nosey and he took too much of the people's money. And then Joe found Joshua at noon standing up in the midst of the preachers, telling them what was what; not as sharply and blusteringly, as Joe would have liked, and yet with a certain assurance and decision that tickled Joe infinitely. He dragged Joshua home, chuckling as he went, in the midst of stern advice.

"You just let them preachers alone. They know lots more than you do, and you can't be sassy to your elders."

Then he would chuckle again and Joshua always remained silent.

And so years went on, ever more swiftly, until there came a question as to what Joshua was going to do for a living after he finished the elementary schools. Joe insisted that he should become a farmer and help him. His mother suggested rather dreamily that he might be a lawyer. Joshua said he was going to be a carpenter and a carpenter he became. A rather good carpenter but slow, and often called away on business of his own. His father's business, he called it.

"It ain't no business of mine," growled Joe.

Then at last Joe began to complain. "First thing you know that fellow is going to be a gangster. He's hanging around with a lot of Communists and talking on street corners, and saying things about property that white folks ain't going to stand for. The police will get after him one of these days and first thing you know he'll be in jail."

But his mother sewed and washed and swept and grew thinner and taller as her eyes grew larger. Only she muttered, as always:

"He is the Son of God."

Once they heard a strange tale from Bethany, a neighboring town. The mob had beat Laz Simmons, one of Joshua's pals, and left him for dead, lying in the gutter. Martha, his sister, ran ten miles to get Joshua and begged him for help when none others dared touch the body. Joshua wept. He bore him home.

"He was nearly dead," said Joe.

"He was dead," said Mary.

"Don't be a fool. He's alive and well."

Mary answered, "He said: 'Laz, get up.' And he got up."

"Yes," sneered Joe, "and them crackers will get Joshua yet for that."

That night Mary went to prayer meeting and shouted before the Lord, waving like a palm in a storm. And as she swayed, she cried with a great voice:

"He is the Resurrection and the Life. He that believeth in Him, though he were dead, yet shall he live!"

Joe didn't like it. Joshua was always out of a job and never had made much money. He didn't dress up, but went about hatless and in old, run-down shoes. He wouldn't get married and didn't seem interested in any of the nice girls; and yet one day he walked down Main Street with Jackson's Babe, a strumpet. Joe nearly struck her when he met them, but Joshua glared at him and they passed on. Joe couldn't figure it out; but boys will be boys, and he remembered that he himself—

Then Joshua kept running with curious people. Outcasts and tramps. Lately he had found a new religion. He was holding meetings and haranging on street corners, and there were white women listening.

Once in curiosity, Joe and Mary slipped down town, and standing apart, shadowed by a tree, listened to Joshua talk. Joe was disappointed to find that the "harangue" which he had heard about was more like teaching. Joshua was sitting on an old fence that ran back of the courthouse and talking to a funny looking crowd:

"Heaven is going to be filled with people who are down-hearted and you that are mourning will get a lot of comfort some day. It's meek folk who are lucky, and going to get everything; and you that are hungry, too. Poor people are better than rich people because they work for what they wear and eat. There won't be any rich people in Heaven. You got to be easy on guys when they do wrong. Then they'll be easy on you, when you get in bad. God's sons are those that won't quarrel. You must treat other people just like you want to be treated. Let'm call you names. Listen! They have called some of the biggest folks that ever lived, dirty names. What's the difference? Which ones do we remember? Don't work all the time. Sit down and rest and sing sometimes. Everthing's all right. Give God time. And say, you know how folks use to think they must get even with their enemies? Well, I'll tell you what: you just love your enemies. And if anybody hits you, don't hit 'em back. Just let them go on beating you—"

"Come on," growled Joe. "I ain't never heard so much damned nonsense since I was borned."

At last Joshua went away on a long journey; he did not say good-bye but cried at the gate.

"Hail, Mary!"

And gripping Joe's hand, was gone. The years heavy-footed rolled on. "He will be 25 today," they said; "Today he will be thirty!" They heard rumors of strange things that he did.

"He may come home rich," growled Joe testily.

But Mary mused.

"He is despised and rejected of men,
A man of sorrows and acquainted with grief."

Then at last it came like a flash in the sky, when the young man was in his early thirties, yet seemed to them still a baby. He had been seized by a mob and they had hanged him at sunset. The charge against him wasn't clear: "Worshipping a new God." "Living with white women!" "Getting up a revolution." "Stealing or blasphemy," the neighbors muttered. Joe came home cursing and half drunk.

"Trying to get out of his place; that's it," he yelled. "Criticizing white folks—I told him—I warned him—"

But Mary left her tub; set aside her broom and laid the thimble and scissors carefully in the machine drawer; she put on her black dress and went into the parlor and sat there in the darkness, tall and stern, with an oil lamp in the window that lit the rigid halo of her hair and threw across the yard the black shadow of a noosed and hanging rope. And Mary said:

"His name shall be called Wonderful, Councillor, the Mighty God, the Ever-Lasting Father and the Prince of Peace."

"You crazy fool," shrieked Joe. "You always was dippy about that idiot."

But Mary talked on.

"Behold the Sign of Salvation—a noosed rope."

Joe flung out of the room and fell down the steps and crawled out to the barn and leaned against it; gripping its planks with bleeding hands.

He saw the shadow of the Noose across the world and heard Mary's voice looming in the night:

"He is the Son of God!"

And Joe buried his head in the dirt and sobbed.

66

A Little Play

Time: Now.
Place: Here.
Enter the Pale One and the Brown One, dressed alike, speaking English, but coming from opposite entrances.

The Pale One: "Colored people are dirty, ignorant, lazy, poor and rude. Until they become clean, intelligent, thrifty, well to do and polite they must expect to be treated badly."

The Brown One: "Are all colored people dirty, ignorant, lazy and rude? If so, I am colored and therefore I must be—"

The Pale One: "Oh, no! I mean most colored people; or at any rate some colored people."

The Brown One: "And therefore should all colored people be treated badly, or only the dirty and ignorant and lazy and poor and rude?"

The Pale One: "Only the dirty and ignorant and—"

The Brown One: "And is it only dirty, ignorant, lazy, poor and rude *colored* folk who are to be badly treated?"

The Pale One: "Certainly not. All people who are dirty, ignorant, lazy, poor and rude must expect bad treatment."

The Brown One: "And has history proven that 'bad treatment' is the best cure for dirt, ignorance, poverty and rudeness, or is bad treatment their cause?"

The Pale One: "I can't go into that. At present they are treated badly."

The Brown One: "They surely are. And now, finally, how shall I be treated?"

The Pale One: "You shan't marry my sister."

The Brown One: "I don't want to; but to return to the subject—"

The Pale One: "You are seeking social equality!"

The Brown One: "If that means I'm seeking decent treatment—"

The Pale One: "You belong to an inferior race!"

The Brown One: "For Heaven's sake—"

The Pale One: "Oh, bother!"

Exit the Pale One in anger.
Exit the Brown One in thought.

From *The Crisis* 7 (March 1914): 241.

67

The Christ of the Andes

Scene I.

Echo. Ximene.

Ximene. Francesco!
   Whence leaps this strange new name
   So coldy to my lips—and that
   Pale bloodless face I seem to see afar,
   So sharp and queer—I hate it.
   Yet how lithe and strong he looks
   How wicked wilful!
   The Gods of the Moluchi grant
   I see him never more!

Atualpa. Greetings, O Daughter of the Moon.
   Father what means this vision?

Huascar. Who are these bloodless ghosts?

Old Man. They are devils that come from
      nether hell
   To torture them that torture their own selves.
   Cease war and murder of thy kin,
   Face these fierce foes
   With grim and undivided strength
   And thy great sinewed arms
   Shall squeeze from out their greed
   The secret of the splendor thou hast viewed.

A. Thus have I ever said
   And say again, but this base brawler here—

H. Peace is my dearest dream, but peace with
      Honor.

From *The Horizon* 4 (November–December 1908): 1–10. [This note preceded the scenes given here: "Two scenes from a drama which with one other received highest mention in a recent competition for a $1,000 prize; the prize was not awarded to either." Du Bois remarked, in a letter to Frank E. Taylor (March 29, 1943), editor-in-chief of the publishing firm Reynal and Hitchcock, that "It was once adjudged the best play submitted for a prize to a peace society in Boston but they reneged on giving me the prize unless I had the play staged, which was of course impossible."—ED.]

This base liar here—

Messenger. Ho! have care—look yonder;
There cometh up the mountain paths
A mighty cloud of men.
Pale as the dead they are and bloodless;
Their limbs be clad in glittering silver,
Long iron clubs lie lightly in their hands,
They sit astride great prancing beasts!
Away! They come!
And murder sits upon
Their sharpened cruel faces!

A. Ho! Save the princess
Away with her to Araucania;
She who hath plead so vainly
With this stark and mad usurper,
For my throne.

Huascar. Ho! Save the princess,
Away with her to Chili;
She who sacredly refuses
To supplant a royal sister!

Atualpa. What! And will thy lips profane
the king's bethrothed?

H. Thou art no king—thou art no man;
Thou art a dog that vomits forth thy rage.
(Enter Spaniards)

A. Ho! thou white and gleaming host,
Help me to kill this false and lying thing
That dares blaspheme an Inca of Peru!

Pizzaro. Right graciously O King!

(The old man leads the princess away. As she turns she sees Francesco and he spies her.)

Francesco. Ximene!

Ximene. Francesco!

(He rushes madly forward, but the whirl of renewed battle bears him back. She disappears.)

Scene 2.

SCENE: A crag surmounted by a fortified Indian Palace closely guarded by silent warriors. The princess enters and sadly looks into Valley and Sea.

Ximene. There sits an awful silence
On the Sea, and o'er the mighty mountains
The hushed air doth creep with weak
And trembling footsteps
The rivers smell of blood
And yonder carrion condor

Drunk on human hearts
Shrieks and wheels up and homeward
To his babes. O fated land!
O vale of Death, O Mother of red murder
And of war—hark!
What roars from out the glen
With human accents? My God they come.
The blasphemy of cursing
Cuts the air.
The muttered mouthings
Of their barrelled thunder knells
From out the dells and echoes and re-echoes
On the vast
Andean shoulders of the hills.
They come, ye gods, they come!
As sweeps the throttled
Bursting anger in the Devil's breast;
As whirls the maddened
Torrent of the Spring
Around that silvery gleaming central core,
Dark, terrible; the soldiering of my great father's realm
Do swarm and sting.
Fond Heaven! How they reel, their death cries
Shake the cliffs and send the eagles
Screaming to the air.
Accursed be the sight—I will not see—
And yet I must, since country, life and hope itself
Hang in the awful scale.
How hateful, harsh, and hideous
Gleam the bloodless masks
On that inhuman host.
Gleam the bloodless masks
On that inhuman host.

  (A band of Spaniards headed by Francesco appears fighting.)

See that great iron-nosed monster far ahead
Who plows with devilish skill
The heart blood of our men—Great Father!
Make me once a man; give me a spear—
Ah! That face; that fearful face!
That pale and bloodless face afar
So sharp and queer—I hate it.
Yet how lithe and strong he looks
How wicked wilful.
He comes! Francesco!
His spear points towards my heart;
His eyes do glisten as the serpent's
Horrid gaze!

  (The battle rages close to the palace gates.)

What Ho, Moluchi:

Fend me—here, there, stand, fight!
Thy princess calls—Father, Brother,
Cousin—
'Round me!
On thy dead souls
That monster dare not woo.

    (A fierce and bitter struggle at the gates.)

Hush.
Eyes, see not!
Ears, hear not!
Heart, lift up thy prayer to God!
  Spirit of wonder
  Daughter of Thunder
 Fire that lurks in the cavernous Sea!
  Mist of the mountain
  Song of the fountain
 Mingle thy might to the guarding of me!
  God of the Day
  Lord of the Way
 Fire that flames for the Child of the Sun,
  Conquer the Terrible
  Vanquish the Horrible
 Pity thy children, Adorable One!

 (She rises from her knees and looks; the main battle has swept onward leaving but Francesco fighting his way to Ximene.)

What new and creeping silence is this now?
I hear the ring of silver—ringing, ringing, ringing!
Far off the echoes of the battle die
As it sweeps past.
But here! Father of mercies—
Here and alone!
All silent
Bloody, wounded,
Torn and terrible: comes—
Francesco!

Francesco. Ximene!

    (The princess' family attack him.)

Ximene. My older brother dies; his hands
 Claw the red earth.
 (What eyes this white-faced monster hath.)
 The head of my great cousin grins
 A yard from his vast shoulders.
 (Oh the dread strength of that long slim white arm;
 How thrills and throbs his thin thrust
 Through the air!)

My; little brother sinks and sighs
As he did sign in sleep. Oh, Oh!
(What wondrous courage this white warrior hath!)
My uncle yells his last great war cry
To the hills.
Lo! the white spirit sways and falls.
God pity him—no—no, yes, O fate, he dies!
Wonder! He staggers up again, his
Great green eyes on me.
What—love must nerve his iron will!
On, on he reels.
My father cuts the silver from his head.
Ah! Ah! Softly—ah softly, Father—
Was that my father once,
That drabbled bloody thing
That spurts its slime on my cold breast?
The gates do yield!

(She steps within the palace doors.)

He comes, nearer, nearer, near—here—
Hear! Hark!

(She closes them)

Francesco. Open, or by Christ the King—

(She opens them and stands within alone.)

Ximene. Francesco!

(He stands panting and swaying on his sword; she recoils.)

F. Ximene!

X. Beast!

F. Woman!

X. (Whispering) I—love thee.

F. Come!

X. (Wildly) And I hate me that I do!
Ah!

(He seizes her in his arms, and carries her into the palace. The doors close. Night falls and the moon rises. The doors open. Francesco appears pale and erect.)

Francesco. How whirls the world!
The mountains dance in drunken revel:
I am so strangely weak.
What's this? Why 'tis blood;
Good red and streaming blood!

(The Old Man appears in the door, Ximene lying stark and bloody across his arms with streaming hair.)

I—Ximene!
Ha! Who art thou
That stands above my wedded wife?
I know thee—ha!
I know thee, Jew—old death's head!
Thou riseth from the grave to mock me.
I fear thee not: I'll kill thee presently again.
Wipe first the trailing blood
From off the princess' bridal gown,
It is not meet—

(Sways and totters, while the Old Man and the maid remain motionless.)

Ha! What?
What sayest thou so silently?
Thou art death?
What have I to do with death?
I am young!
I am strong!
I am wed!
Art thou Death?
Then I'll kill thee, Death,
And live forever!
Grip fast thy scythe,
Defend!
One, two—
Coward, dost thou run:
Thinkest thou thus to escape Saaveedra's
mighty sword?
Unhand me! Off with thy cold wet hands!
Knave, base-born, unknightly, caitiff!
Unhand me I say,
Or by the great King I'll run thee through!
I'll—
What! callest thou Witchery to darken all the World
In this bright morning hour?
Thy magic all be damned;
I'll grope thee out thro' blackness ten times
blacker than the blackest hell!
Take that—and that—and that;
I warned thee fair.

What Ho! Ximene!
Death is dead
We'll live forever!

(Crashes to the earth and dies.)

CURTAIN.